After You Have Suffered A While

An Autobiography

Tracy Fowler

But the God of all grace, who hath called us unto his eternal glory by Christ Jesus, after that ye have suffered a while, make you perfect, stablish, strengthen, settle you.
1 Peter 5:10 KJV

After You Have Suffered A While
Copyright © 2021 by Tracy Fowler

All rights reserved. No part of this book may be reproduced or transmitted in any form or by any means without written permission from the author.

Photos are from the author's private collection.

All scriptures are taken from the King James Version (KJV) of the Holy Bible which is in the public domain.

Scripture taken from the New King James Version®. Copyright © 1982 by Thomas Nelson. Used by permission. All rights reserved.

The Holy Bible, New International Version (NIV) copyright © 1973, 1978, 1984, 2011 by Biblica, Inc. Used by permission. All rights reserved.

Published by:
Claire Aldin Publications
P.O. Box 453 Southfield, MI 48037
www.clairealdin.com

Library of Congress Number 2021918705

ISBN 978-1-954274-04-4 paperback
ISBN 978-1-954274-06-8 eBook

Printed in the United States of America.

Dedication

This book is dedicated to Mrs. Patricia Buehrig, my twelfth-grade English teacher. She made us keep journals and told me that I should get published one day. Thank you for validating me and giving me a voice. You were the best English teacher ever!

Table of Contents

Introduction 7

Chapter 1 – My Chocolate Chunk 11

Chapter 2 – My Reason to Rise 33

Chapter 3 – Above and Beyond 45

Chapter 4 – I know Love 87

Chapter 5 - Hater 101

Chapter 6 – My Stuff 177

Chapter 7 - Friendship 185

Chapter 8 – Why Do The Righteous Suffer? 221

Chapter 9 – Somebody Cared 251

All scripture is given by inspiration of God, and is profitable for doctrine, for reproof, for correction, for instruction in righteousness:
2 Timothy 3:16 KJV

Introduction

My life has been wrought with pain and disappointment. If I ever doubted that I was saved, I don't anymore. I know that I know *that I know*. I am already seated in heavenly places in Christ Jesus. Some of my experiences were so disturbing, that I've journaled about them and turned them into poetry in efforts to make sense of the trauma and drama. I used to internalize the hateful words and behavior inflicted upon me by relatives and coworkers. Those demons I saw on my job were the same demons I saw not only in the people I loved, but also within some church members. That was devastating!

As a result, I fell into depression. My hair fell out. I slept too long. I couldn't sleep. I ate too much. I couldn't eat. I cried. *A lot*. I got angry. I overspent, trying to fill voids that only Jesus could fill.

"Lord, why?" I questioned. I practiced my pain instead of the Lord's presence. I struggled to get it together. For years.

*Suffering persecution is being maltreated by others because you are a true disciple of Christ. It includes being falsely accused, unjustly condemned or imprisoned, being ridiculed, scorned, rejected, or injured. Persecution is not suffering for doing wrong toward others, or for disobeying rightful authority.

Through counseling and prayer, I realized that there was a demon in my midst—a destroyer demon. This thing was here to desecrate my character. He was not here because I was a bad person. This demon was here because I was saved and was a threat to him. One day, I was on a friend's social media page. He was a young man I'd met at a friend's wedding when I was in college over thirty years before. He liked me and wanted us to be more than friends. At that time, I would always bring possible suiters to church. If you wanted to date me, you had to know my Jesus! This young man and I did not hit it off. He started seeing another young lady in the congregation soon after, whom he later married. Today, he pastors his own church. I was listening to them sing a praise song together. His wife has the most beautiful voice! I couldn't stop smiling at the thought that the Lord allowed me to witness to him, and now he has been impacting God's kingdom for many years-reaching many converts for Christ. That day, I needed to see that. It served as a reminder that my life has been worth something. That my living and suffering were not in vain.

Satan knows that he could never keep me out of heaven, but if he caused confusion and rendered me ineffective—then what good was I to my children, or to anyone else that God wanted me to impact for His glory?

My pastor once preached, "There are four ways you can tell if you have a demon in your life."

1. This person is close in proximity—a relative, coworker, and/or friend (enemy in disguise).
2. They're deceitful.
3. They never admit to any wrongdoing.
4. They're treacherous.

I know several people who embody all four characteristics. But know this: The Christian's life has a victorious ending. We win! I am winning! Despite Satan's attempts to destroy me, I know who I am, and *whose* I am. This changed the way I looked at my life. The anger and hopelessness dissipated, and I felt free! Finally, free. I was not the bad guy. *They* were. And I was not going to let them steal my joy anymore.

God uses our pain to perfect us. Just look at the lives of Joseph and Job. Joseph made it to the palace by way of the pit, Potiphar's house, and prison. Despite the betrayal he suffered, Joseph remained faithful to the Lord, and the Lord blessed him to become the second in command in all of Egypt. Joseph forgave those who had betrayed him. Job was a billionaire by today's standards. God allowed Satan to take all that Job had—his wealth, his children, and his health. Nevertheless, God restored his health, and all that he'd had two-fold (Job

42:10). According to the Ryrie Study Bible[1], "unmerited tragedy helps us see God, which is unmerited grace."

This is my story chronicling years of suffering. Decades of *going through*. My hope is that if you are going through any of what I have been through, you will find encouragement and help for your journey.

Chapter One

My Chocolate Chunk

7/29/1997

Two years ago, we said "I do!"

How could you know that I'd love you?

Despite my nagging, hagging way,
With me I hope you'll always stay.
You are so generous, so loving, so kind.

Your admitted flaws I do not mind.
You are so honest, so godly, so smart,
it is no wonder you stole my heart.
There are many reasons why I admire you so much.

Could it be your gentle touch

That sends all aches floating away?

That makes the invisible hairs stand up and
say, YES! This feels great! Could it be the ease
in which you've accepted fatherhood without a
twitch? You handle our son with so much care,
it's comforting to know you'll always be there,
for him, for me, for us.

You do it all without a fuss.

No matter what I've said before,
or what I'll say tomorrow more, I
love you Jeff, so don't ever forget,
marrying you I'll never regret.
You were born to marry me didn't
you know, can't you see?
Happy, Happy Anniversary!

Jeffery Bryant Fowler and I met in the ninth grade. We were in English class together and became fast friends. He was the defensive tackle on the football team. A childhood friend nicknamed him "Truck." He once had a bicycle that had a steering wheel instead of handlebars. His friend said it looked like he was driving a truck when he rode his bike, so the name stuck. Occasionally, Jeffery would walk me almost the whole way home from school. He wasn't silly like so many of the other boys in high school. He was mature and so smart! We could talk about anything. Our talks became an entry or two in my high school journal.

Jeffery was always a gentleman. Never made a pass at me, never even asked me out. Then one evening during our eleventh-grade year, he called me.

"Hi Tracy, I baked you a chocolate cake. Come and get it!"

What? This big football-playing dude baked? A cake? *For me*? It wasn't Valentine's Day or my birthday. It wasn't any special day at all. My mom drove me to his house. I met his mom and his younger brother. Jeffery unceremoniously gave me the cake.

"Thanks Jeff!" I said, and back home we went. Mom made me return the gesture, by demanding that we bake him a cake. Ugh! She did not know how to accept kindness without having to outdo folks.

Boys, to me, were, *eh*. I wasn't one of those fast, loose girls in high school. I had one boyfriend for a few months. We were both fifteen when he asked me to have sex with him. After I angrily refused, he kicked me out of his house and told me never to return. That exchange solidified my belief of boys being the biggest jerks in the world.

Outside of the occasional dance partner at quarter parties around the way, our relationship never passed the friendship threshold. However, Jeffery would later tell me that he was in love with me in high school but was too afraid to tell me, for fear of rejection. After high school, we lost touch. We were each trying to find our own way and follow our own paths.

It was the summer of our ten-year high school reunion. Two friends and I had gone to the grocery store, and who do I run into but Jeffery! We hugged, asked how each other was doing, and exchanged phone numbers. He later told me that the cashier commented that he must really like me 'cause he kept cheesin'. He told her, "She's going to be my wife one day." Talk about *faith*!

Jeffery called me the next day, and our friendship picked up where it had left off. He was easy to be with. Handsome, articulate, very friendly, and giving. There were no pretenses. I didn't have to always look my best when he showed up. And he didn't complain. He was a breath of fresh air. We were twenty-eight, and we both had been around the block a time or two. I'd had my heart broken already and had starred in my own version of the 1977 movie, Looking for Mister Goodbar, without the tragic ending, of course. Looking for love in all the wrong places, I had kissed plenty of frogs on the road to finding and *appreciating* my prince.

Jeffery quickly told me he wanted more than a friendship. Now, it's not what you think. He just didn't want to hear me talk anymore of past relationships. After all, he'd moved out of the house he was sharing with a young lady, to move back in with his mother in order to be closer to me. Ladies, when a man loves you — truly loves you, he will change his address if he can.

At that time, I was attending Bible study at a church different from my home church. The young preacher who taught Bible study blew me away! For the first time, a man of God was so transparent! In front of us—including his pretty, pregnant wife, he divulged his struggles, past and present, as a saved Christian man. His transparency drew me in. He was funny and deep, all at the same time. I felt like the woman in the Bible, who after talking with Jesus, said "Come, see a man, which told me all things that ever I did..." (John 4:29 KJV).

Jesus was revealing Himself to me. Finally, I was learning who the Father, Son, and the Holy Spirit really were. I didn't have to be perfect; I needed to be obedient and willing to work to perfection. I'd been in church all my life and was in ministry even as a young girl during my elementary school years. I was a tithe payer, but I still had not really comprehended this Christianity thing until then.

I eventually left my church and joined this one with the serious yet transparent, friendly, young preacher. Whenever Jeffery came over, my sister and I would eagerly share what we were learning at Truth Bible Institute. This was serious. We had papers to write, and tests to take. And we loved it! Jeffery would hang on our every word. He'd been raised Muslim and started going to a Baptist church after his parents divorced. He'd not really settled in on Jesus Christ as Savior. But God was using me to witness to him.

It's funny when I think of it. When I was in college, I dated a young man who I graduated high school with. After a while, he mentioned that he was thinking about converting to Islam. I didn't take him seriously at first. I mean, he dressed way too flamboyant to ditch his digs for a kufi and traditional garments. Have you ever seen a male peacock with his tail feathers expanded? This guy didn't strut like a peacock, but his clothes were so different, and so fly. And his tall, slender build made everything he wore that much more dope. He had a pair of shoes to match every outfit. Everywhere we went, people commented on his clothes. I was waiting for somebody to ask him, "What are you doing with *her*?"

Have you ever seen a female peacock? That was me. Bland, and un-fly. Jeans, flats, and a shirt—you know, the average college student uniform. He wanted me to convert so we could get married. I went to the Masjid with him. The men sat in chairs up front. The women sat on the floor in the back. *Nooo*. Nope. They let me sit in a chair in the back. I had on a red skirt and red flats. I could not have felt more out of place. We had constant debates on Christianity versus Islam. He'd invited a Muslim friend of his on our dates to try to convince me. My mother would join in. No daughter of hers was gonna become Muslim. In the end, we parted ways. He converted and married a Muslim woman, and I held on to my Jesus. Alone.

Jeffery wooed me. Our thing was to fill up the gas tank in his truck and get on a road and ride it to see where it took us. We loved to go for long rides, and we enjoyed long walks on the beach and the boardwalk. He bought me roses and wrote poetry. I would come home from work to find a dozen roses in my door — each week. Some mornings as I approached my car to go to work, there would be a poem or love note folded up on my windshield.

Jeffery was so smart, and also a good listener. I once lamented about having to give up my Barbie dolls when I was a teenager. Wouldn't you know that Barbie, her townhouse, her Corvette, and even Ken were sitting in my door on different days when I came home from work? He was full of surprises! Jeffery took flying lessons and even piloted a plane! Whenever a plane flew overhead, he would yell out the make and model of that plane. He had wanted to be an air force pilot when he was growing up.

It was as if God had pressed the pause button on my brokenness, to show me His love for me. True love is not expensive. Does not require anyone to break the bank. If he/she is pressing you to spend all your money on him/her, he/she ain't the one. Two years after we bumped into each other at the grocery store, he asked me to marry him. Yes! I wore my beautiful engagement ring like a badge of honor!

Jeffery was a senior corrections officer at a state prison. Since he worked on Sundays, he could not attend church with me. Even though he had not been baptized yet, he would give me ten percent of his earnings to put into the plate as his tithes. God was truly working on his heart.

I've realized that some people just do not like to see you happy. All while we were dating, my family loved Jeffery. He was the only guy that my brother James liked of all the dudes I had brought home. But once we got engaged, my mother openly questioned my love for him. She began to pick him apart. Dumb, superficial things. What made our union difficult was that these people were close to us. Or should I say, close to me. Other people began to throw up stuff that had me explaining our love and relationship. I was weak-minded back then. I cared too much about what people thought. The *wrong* people. So, after four months, I gave him his ring back. What a dork I was. He was devastated. He told me that I was "the best whoever did it."

"Be who you are and say what you think, cause those who matter don't mind, and those who mind don't matter."

Dr. Seuss

There were plenty of women at my church who were eager to un-break his heart. And he found one. Jeffery no longer worked Sundays, so he was able to attend Sunday services, Wednesday night Bible study, and other church events. How awkward it was to run into him and his new boo all the time. She was older than us. The first time Jeffery attended this church, he was with me; however, everybody began to know him as one half of a couple with *her*. I missed his baptism. I missed him getting the right hand of fellowship after completing discipleship classes. What a dork I was.

A year later, I was lying in bed thinking about what I was going to wear to church. It was a Sunday morning. The phone rang and when I answered it, my mother was crying hysterically. In between sobs, she said that my brother James had been in an accident and was in the hospital. She wanted my sister and I to come over. I jumped out of bed, ran into my sister's room and told her what my mother had said. We clasped hands and began to pray earnestly for our brother. We did not know the particulars, but we knew it wasn't good.

When we got to my mother's house, she was prostrate on the floor, crying and praying. A friend of the family stood over her trying to comfort her. She told us to take care of our mother and she left. She was affiliated with my brother's karate school. As the day went by, relatives, friends, and church members filled my mother's house as she spoke on the phone with the hospital and with my brother's sensei. The accident took place in North Carolina. We lived in New Jersey, so they were trying to arrange a flight for my parents to get to the hospital. My brother had been helicoptered to the trauma unit and was on life support.

I was six years old when my brother James was born. My sister and I would help our mother with feeding him his bottle and changing his diapers. He was like a little doll baby. So cute! Big eyes with long, curly eyelashes. He had a lot of hair that my mom kept braided. One day, I was pushing him up and down the street in his stroller when a couple leaned down to admire him. It was summertime, and all he had on was a diaper.

"She is so cute!" the lady exclaimed.

"He's a boy, not a girl!" I angrily retorted. *How could this grown lady be so stupid*, I thought to myself.

By the time James started walking, we had nicknamed him "Little Man." He just seemed to be more mature for his age. Sure-footed, helpful, and a born leader. He was very meticulous. One evening, he was crying profusely. My mom had put him to bed and asked him why he was so upset.

"I got a hole in my pajamas!" he wailed. Oh boy, did we crack up. My mom told him if he did not get back in the bed.

All my girlfriends thought my little brother was so cute. James was the typical little brother. When I was a teen, I caught him once hiding under the bed listening to my conversation with a boy from school. He ran downstairs and told my mom what I had said before I could catch him.

One of the fondest memories I have of my brother, was when he would introduce me to his friends. He would put his hands over my face, as if to say, my sister is cute, *don't try nothing*. That was a big boost to my extremely low self-esteem. No one had ever told me I was attractive.

James and our brother John were twelve months apart. They were partners in crime. Those two were inseparable growing up and were awfully close! When James went to Georgia for the karate tournament, John was living in Georgia. They spent some time together while he was there.

We were all praying and hoping. The hospital called and wanted my mother's permission to donate his organs.

"No!" she exclaimed. Things did not look so good. My parents left for North Carolina.

James and his best friend had driven to Atlanta to compete in a national karate tournament. James was a brown belt, and exceptionally good. His friend, the driver of the car, was a multiple degree black belt. James' sensei trained cadets in the police academy. When James was on life support in North Carolina, his sensei worked it out so that my brother John was driven by state police to the Georgia state line, and then to the North Carolina hospital James had been helicoptered to. He was there with our parents.

On the way back home, James' friend had fallen asleep at the wheel. They hit the concrete wall and the car caught on fire. The driver behind them happened to have a fire extinguisher, and put the fire out before it spread, and did any real harm. My brother was reclined in the passenger seat. His friend's feet were crushed.

The next day, we all gathered at my grandmother's house. She lived right next door to my mom. We were waiting for my parents to call her and tell her of James' progress. They decided to take him off life support. He was dead. His back had been broken, along with other injuries he had sustained. My mother believed he had died at the scene of the accident, and that they had placed him on life support to keep his organs warm if they were to be donated. She made it noticeably clear that his organs had better be in his body when it got to the undertaker.

James was a handsome, healthy twenty-four-year-old. It was obvious that he took particularly good care of himself. Just four days prior, he had asked if I would give him a ride to his friend's house in Philly so they could drive down to Atlanta for the weekend. We were outside my mom's house after work, and I remember telling him to ask mom because I was tired. She can use my car, I told him. If only I had known that that would be the last time I would lay eyes on him alive. Our last conversation. If I had known, I would have hugged him hard and never let him go. My mom and I hopped in my car and drove to my house. We were sitting at the kitchen table when James called. He did not need a ride after all. I heard my mom tell him to be careful and that she loved him.

James had won first place trophies. They were damaged in the accident, but his sensei arranged with the officials of the tournament to have them replaced. They presented them to my mother in a surprising tribute at his burial. A year after the accident, his friend the driver, held a tribute in my brother's honor at his father's karate school. We all attended except for my sister. It was a nice ceremony. He died several years later of walking pneumonia. He had left the hospital before he was discharged. His mother told my mom that he never stopped blaming himself for his friend's death. What a tragedy all the way around.

Jeffery came over every day leading up to the funeral. James always liked Jeffery. All four of my brothers did. He was the only guy I had dated that James liked. I had broken Jeffery's heart and here he was comforting me during this extremely painful moment. He came to the funeral. Weeks after the funeral, Jeffery and John came to get all of James' trophies to take them to my mother's house. Every time James won a tournament, he would bring his six-foot-tall trophies to the house my sister and I shared. We were so proud of him! Now they were taking the trophies away.

I asked Jeffery out on a date on that day. He told me that he was looking forward, and not back. Ouch! I gave the concert tickets I had to my parents.

What God has joined together, let no man put asunder.

A year later, Jeffery called me out of the blue and asked if I wanted to go to the movies. He and his girlfriend had broken up. I had not dated since before my brother died. My brother's death knocked all the foolishness out of me, and I plunged myself into Bible study, Sunday school teaching, and everything else my ever-growing church had to offer. By November, we were engaged again (he still had the engagement ring) and planned a July wedding.

A few weeks before our wedding, the house that my sister and I shared was broken into. My sister and I had spent the weekend at our parents' house. She returned home before I did to find the backdoor wide open, and the kitchen window was smashed. She called me and the police. I got back home to find the thieves had stolen among other things, my brother's leather jacket, my sister's leather jacket, my gold earrings, and money from off my dresser. All my shoe boxes had been opened, and my bedroom ransacked. But laying in plain view on my bed were our wedding bands. The thieves had removed the jewelry store bag from the bottom shelf of my side table, opened the boxes and dumped both rings onto the bed, but for some reason had not taken them. They cost more than the two leather coats, and both pair of gold earrings combined. But there they laid. I thanked God for His divine intervention. Whenever I get down, I am always reminded of events like this. Supernatural things that made no sense and yet worked in our favor.

Jeffery took care of finding us a house and the honeymoon. I took care of the wedding, with my mother's help. And what a wedding it was! All of my siblings were part of the wedding party including my youngest brother, whose birthday happened to fall on that last Saturday of July. He turned ten years old that day. He was dressed in a tuxedo to escort one of my students down the aisle. They were so cute! My wedding cake baker baked a cake for him in the shape of a football to commemorate his birthday, which I presented to him at the reception.

We honeymooned in Maui. Our airplane pilot gave my husband a bottle of champagne as a wedding gift. I had fallen asleep, weary of the day's events. Earlier that day, as we got off the plane for an hour layover in California, my long, manicured, ring fingernail got caught in a metal tube on one of the seats. Took my whole nail off! I cried like a baby as Jeffery searched for a store that sold a first aid kit. Our initial flight from Philadelphia International Airport had been delayed an hour for mechanical reasons. So, we missed our connecting flight in Chicago. We'd waited three hours at Chicago O'Hare International Airport for our next flight to California, on a different airline.

When we had finally made it to Maui, our luggage was a no show. The airline gave us toiletry bags to hold us over until our luggage arrived the next day. We did not need our clothes. Ooh la-la! We had never had sex with each other prior to our honeymoon, hadn't even come close. What an amazingly powerful experience it is to have sex for the first time with someone you love who is your *spouse*! No guilt, no worries. Just pure unadulterated joy!

Marriage is honourable in all, and the bed undefiled: but whoremongers and adulterers God will judge.
Hebrews 13:4 KJV

    A year later, our son was born and fourteen months later, our daughter was born. When I was pregnant with our daughter, Jeffery found out he had renal failure. He needed a kidney transplant. He had been in and out of the hospital ever since we got married. He had high blood pressure and now a failing kidney. Right after my daughter's birth, Jeffery was extremely ill. He couldn't move. He couldn't eat. I was running a bed pan tending to him, feeding our newborn every two hours, and trying to keep our cranky one year old happy. In the midst of all of that, I interviewed for the high school math teacher job at the school two blocks away from our house. I got the job!

    The nephrologist and family doctor Jeffery had at the time were jerks. My mother and I practically carried my husband into the doctor's office, and they both argued with me when I demanded that Jeffery be admitted into the hospital. He was not getting any better laying in the bed at home. He needed medical attention. I had no idea what was wrong with him.

When I asked the nephrologist what renal failure meant, he told me to go to his office and read a pamphlet. *Really?*

Once my husband was discharged after seven days in the hospital, we found out that his kidney had shut down. Instead of putting him on dialysis, the #@%*& nephrologist prescribed two shopping bags of chemicals/medicine. What in the world? All that did was create unwanted side effects and sent him into a depression. Jeffery spent four months at home on disability. Eventually I talked Jeffery into getting two new doctors. He was late to his first appointment with the new nephrologist, so he had to reschedule. On his way home, the nephrologist called me to tell me that he'd looked at my husband's records. He informed me that his creatine levels were so high, he wondered how he had not had a stroke.

"What did the previous nephrologist do?" the new nephrologist asked.

I told him the whole story of that jerk. He said that he wanted my husband to call him as soon as he walked through the door. He was going to have a shunt placed in his arm the Monday after Thanksgiving, which was just a few days away.

"I'll let him enjoy the holiday, but afterwards, he will start dialysis three times a week for four hours each day," he said. "After all, he said, your husband is young, and needs to be around to see his children grow up." He placed my husband on the kidney donor list immediately. Thank you, Jesus! We have a decent doctor now!

For eight months, my husband was on dialysis. It took a lot out of him, but he was a champ. Then he got the call. They had a kidney perfectly matched to him. Yes Lord! Thank you for answering our prayers. Just the day before, he'd found out that his father had passed away. We went to the hospital to get him prepared for surgery. Around midnight, they wheeled him into surgery. They told me they would call me when it was over.

I got the call around 3:00 A.M. Jeffery was in recovery doing fine. The next day, I went to see him. Roommates would come and go over the next few weeks. Men who had the same surgery would heal and walk out to rejoin their families. However, my husband was bleeding from his rectum.

They did a colonoscopy to pinpoint the problem, which warranted another surgery. A temporary colostomy bag. Over time, my husband grew weaker. He took walks down the hall but had to stop and sit. I kept praying and believing.

"Honey, you are going to have an awesome testimony when you get out of here," I would say to him. But a week later he was placed in ICU. There was a bar over his bed that he used to pull himself up. This gentle giant of a man that I'd once witnessed stand flat-footed on my back porch, reach over onto my neighbor's porch, and singlehandedly lift a claw-foot tub, hoist it over his shoulder, walk down the steps, and hoist it gently onto his flatbed truck, was now having a hard time lifting himself.

The ICU nurses told me to bring my children up to see him. I knew children weren't allowed in ICU, but I brought them anyway. Surely my husband isn't going to die. It had been just six years since my brother's death. I could not go through that kind of pain again. *Lord, I know you got this. Right?*

I spent the next night with him in ICU. The nurses put a chair and small TV next to his bed. I didn't sit or watch television. I talked to my husband. The meds took him in and out of consciousness. The next night, I was back at his bedside to be with him through the night. He yelled out in pain. The nurses and a doctor I didn't recognize ran to his side, and they asked me to leave. Several minutes later when I returned, he was resting and the colostomy bag was no longer empty.
I thought to myself, *well that's a good sign. Right?*

My husband woke up a few times to say different things. He pointed to the foot of his bed, eyes closed, and asked calmly, "What's *he* doing here?" "Who?" I asked.

"That little boy." I looked to where he pointed.

"Honey, I don't see a little boy, what does he look like?"

I'd heard stories of people seeing angels on their death bed, and as much as I didn't want to believe it, my husband was seeing his death angel. A little boy dressed in all black.

Nevertheless, I held onto hope, believing that my husband was going to get better. I had felt a tremendous amount of peace on my way to the hospital. The next morning when my husband tried to pull the breathing tube out of his throat with his eyes still shut, I burst into tears. The nurse quietly told me to go home, rest and come back later. I picked up the children from my mother-in-law's house and gave her an update. Then, I went to my sister's house, which was close to the hospital.

The anesthesiologist called to ask permission for another surgery—a permanent colostomy bag.

"Yes, do whatever it takes to save his life!" I said. I napped for an hour or two when my mother-in-law called to tell me that his heart gave out, and that they were working to revive him. When I arrived, they wouldn't let me in the ICU, as they were still working to revive him. He hadn't had the surgery because of his breathing. My mother-in-law was crying, and I was frantic. Then, the surgeon who performed the kidney transplant walked out. He looked at me sadly and shook his head. I collapsed on the floor.

My thirty-seven-year-old husband died of sepsis when his bowel was perforated during the kidney transplant. Negligence? Four different law firms would say no. My husband's death was a bitter pill I just had to swallow. He was a walking deacon and faithful member of the outreach ministry. A faithful tithe payer, great husband, and an excellent father who didn't mind changing diapers.

Affectionately called "Terminator" by his co-workers at the prison, the inmates at his prison held a memorial service for him. Jeffery treated the inmates like humans. Like men. And they respected him. The flag at Riverfront State Prison flew at half-staff in his memory. His fellow officers were his pallbearers. Busses from three different prisons carried officers to the funeral to pay their last respects to this gentle giant of a man.

My pastor came off his vacation to eulogize my husband. Acts 16:23-40 was the scripture text for his eulogy. Both my brother and husband were good men. Good people. Their deaths just didn't seem fair, and it still doesn't. God was a stranger to me for a long time afterwards. I was numb. I felt that I was being punished for all the wrong I had done. Jeffery died August 25, 1999. Our son was five days shy of his third birthday. Our daughter was twenty-one months old.

Chapter Two

My Reason to Rise

3/29/02

I don't often feel a reason to get out of bed, with all
my worries and ills swimming in my head. But the
sun drops down and hits me on my face, bringing
a new day of God's mercy and grace.
Slowly, reluctantly, I open up my
eyes, And there they are, my two
reasons to rise.

I started graduate school eleven days after I buried my husband. I had already registered. The first class started just four days after his funeral, but I needed more time. I was battling depression. All I wanted to do was hide under the covers. But I had two young human beings whose lives depended on me. I had to grow up quickly. I was grown, but I really had to mature and snap out of the growing depression that my overwhelming life was steeped in. I was mad at God, but I asked Him to keep me. Keep me from cursing Him. Keep me from acting out of anger and hurt. Keep me from punching folks in the face who'd pissed me off.

So then faith cometh by hearing, and hearing by the word of God.
Romans 10:17 KJV

The LORD is nigh unto them that are of a broken heart; and saveth such as be of a contrite spirit. Psalm 34:18 KJV

When you are going through tribulation and reeling from trauma, the best thing to do is *pray*. Talk to God and be honest about how you feel. He loves us immensely! He already knows our thoughts anyway, so be honest with Him.

Not forsaking the assembling of ourselves together, as the manner of some is; but exhorting one another: and so much the more, as ye see the day approaching.
Hebrews 10:25 KJV

I kept going to church. The best two hours of my week was Sunday morning worship service. It was my kryptonite! Whatever I was thinking or feeling, God spoke on it through my pastor's sermons. Everything that pertained to me was laid out in plain English. I had the victory over my circumstances! I did not have to be a victim. People were not gonna allow that anyway.

The devil kicks you when you're down. Some people didn't care that I had suffered a major tragedy. They were mean and nasty. My principal at the time, made an announcement at a faculty meeting, appealing the staff to take up a collection for me, and they did. Usually when something happens, the chairperson in your department initiates a collection and passes a card around. People had had surgeries, babies, etc., and I gave to those causes. Now that it was my turn to benefit, my department did nothing. God Bless you, Mr. Harmelin!

"For I know the thoughts that I think toward you, saith the LORD, thoughts of peace, and not of evil, to give you an expected end.
Jeremiah 29:11 KJV

I typed this verse in a very large font on 8 ½ by 11-inch paper and taped it to the wall by my bed. It was the first thing I read each morning, and the last thing I read at night. Satan was trying to convince me that God didn't love me and that I was being punished. But the Lord was saying that His thoughts of me were of *peace,* and not evil. He had an *expected end* for my life. An expectancy and a hope—the things that I longed for. Wow! What an awesome promise from the lover of our soul! I couldn't see the light at the end of the tunnel. My life felt like a nightmare. But I had to believe that God had a better plan for me than the one I was living.

I was way too busy to mourn the tragic loss I'd just suffered. Whoever said that God does not give us more than we can bear, lied. Just look at the life of Paul after his conversion.

We are perplexed, but not in despair; persecuted, but not forsaken; struck down, but not destroyed -- always carrying about in the body the dying of the Lord Jesus, that the life of Jesus also may be manifested in our body. For we who live are always delivered to death for Jesus' sake, that the life of Jesus also may be manifested in our mortal flesh.
2 Corinthians 4:8-12 NKJV

But you have carefully followed my doctrine, manner of life, purpose, faith, longsuffering, love, perseverance, persecutions, afflictions, which happened to me at Antioch, at Iconium, at Lystra what persecutions I endured. And out of them all the Lord delivered me.
2 Timothy 3:10-11 NKJV

After two months, I went back to work. High school math teacher by day, mommy of two toddlers at night. Teenagers and toddlers! Whew! In between all of that craziness was my graduate studies. Meetings with my study group, going to the local college to look at microfiche for research, late night paper writing, and all-day Saturday classes, with the occasional mid-week evening class. Not to mention the paperwork that comes with being a teacher—lesson plans, grading assessments, etc. Whew! Those years are a blur to me now. Thank you Jesus I went *through* it and didn't stay stuck in it!

Three and Four

(2/7/01)

When you smile, the sun comes out when you laugh, the birds sing and shout when you dance, the trees boogaloo when you run, I take off behind you you've learned so much in so little time you wear me out, make me whine I love you simply because you're you not because of the things you do you are the product of a love that was

knowing that you're mine, gives me a
buzz when you smile, the sun comes out
and when you laugh my heart begins to shout!

Advocate for your Children!

Way before I married and had children, I did a biblical study on the word *power*. I came across one of the Hebrew words for power, *chayil*. If you've read the story of Gideon, where God called him a mighty man of "valor," you've come across the name Chayil. The Hebrew word for valor is Chayil. I told myself that if I ever have a son, I would bless him with that name. It just so happened that my awesome husband, who's now with the Lord, didn't mind his firstborn not being named after him.

When our skinny, five-pound, thirteen-ounce baby boy came into the world, he was anything but Chayil—strength, might, ability, force, army. As a matter of fact, he had developmental delays, and has struggled to do everything. As if things weren't bad enough, his neurologist gave me more harrowing news when he was thirteen. He seemed to be regressing, and I'd nearly lost hope. But God! What I didn't see at first was that my man-child was being strengthened daily by life's disappointments and setbacks. God doesn't strengthen us with a life of ease, he strengthens us through tribulation, trauma, and trials! My son has had his fair share of all these. And as we watched him step up to the podium and accept his diploma, we were assured that the "Lord is with thee, thou mighty man of valor."

Our son was late. At least that's what our calculations told us. He was due August 17th. But when that day came and left, I got a little concerned. Maybe we were wrong. At any rate, this child in my womb whose little legs never seemed to stop moving inside of me, was not moving anywhere near the exit chute. The constant fluttering left me confident he was okay but concerned enough to let the doctor talk me into scheduling an induction on the twenty ninth.

They set me up to a Pitocin drip from 12:00 a.m. 'til 6:00 p.m. when little man began his descent into the world. My doctor gave me an episiotomy. Either she was in a hurry or there were complications I wasn't aware of. She cut me from the roota to the toota. When the epidural wore off, the pain from being cut was unbearable. If I had to do it over again, I would have just waited for him to come out on his own. They always do eventually. He was screaming his head off as he entered the world. I can't say that I blame him.

Our son looked like a Martian at birth. He was not all the way done. It was too early. About twelve hours after his birth, around 5 a.m. the morning after I delivered him, a nurse stopped by my room with my son in a crib on wheels so I could walk him to the Intensive Care Nursery (ICN). He couldn't keep an ounce of milk down, and he was hypoglycemic. He spent four days in the ICN.

I cried like a baby when they told me I couldn't take my baby home. Those four days seemed like an eternity. He was losing weight instead of gaining, and he was already so tiny. They said that they didn't know what was wrong with him. They were going to take him to Children's Hospital of Philadelphia (CHOP).

We prayed and prayed. The bottom of my son's tiny feet had several needle marks. Why are they sticking him so much? On the fourth day, they called and told me he could come home, but I had to stop and get a preemie nipple for him. I didn't question this odd request. Afterall, this was a hospital and the intensive care for newborn premature babies. Shouldn't they have their own preemie nipples?

I heaped so much love on my son when we got him home. He even slept in the bed with my husband and I most nights. I would not let him out of my sight. We spoiled him—no, we just loved him deeply. He was a joy, and hilarious! When he was a toddler, he loved imitating our pastor. After church, he'd stand in the middle of the living room and preach. We didn't know what he was saying, but based on his animated movements and inflections, we knew he was repeating what he'd heard. He would crack us up!

When my son was five, he was classified multiply disabled. My husband had been instrumental in signing him up for early intervention when he was two. I was in denial. My son's slow progress in doing everything wasn't a big deal to me.

"Leave my baby alone. He's alright. He will do it when he's ready."

With two RN's in the family—my grandmother, who was retired, and my mother-in-law, both of whom were probably in my husband's ear with their observations, he decided to make the call without my input. After an interview by two women who were elated that the father had so much knowledge about his child, my son was in the program. I was unable to make the meeting because of an after-school program I participated in.

My husband was an exceptionally good father. When his kidney failed him after our daughter's birth, he was out on disability for four months. He was at home with my grandmother each weekday, helping her tend to the children.

If he hadn't videotaped our babies at that time, I would not have any videos of them when they were babies.

The elementary school was right around the corner from our house. Days after my husband's death, my son started public school in the pre-school handicapped disabled class for half the day. He would be in this class for two years before he started full-day kindergarten. When he was five, I was transferred to his school as the math coach. The school district I was teaching in dissolved, and they did not need as many math teachers at the high school. Since I had the least tenure, they sent me down the street. Same town, different school district.

My son and I, and eventually my daughter, would walk into school together each morning. What a blessing! For me anyways. Not so much for my bothered coworkers. In the spring of that first year, his teacher brought her class to the library. My five-year-old son saw me in my office working with a group of students. He waved and said, "Hi, Mommy!" I waved and said hi as his teacher pulled out a chair and made him sit. His little head went down on the table. *Did she just put my baby in time out? For saying hi to his mother?* Good thing this happened at the end of the day because I was livid! I couldn't get around to her room fast enough at dismissal. She was ignorantly defensive.

"My job is to teach him social skills," she retorted.

"And my job as his mother is to make sure his self-esteem is intact."

"Well, I did not want him to disturb you."

I told this childless older woman that if I were a college professor in a lecture hall with five hundred students and my son walked by, I would excuse myself and greet my son. My son is more important to me than any other child in that school, because when I teach my last class, and my career is over, I will still be his mother! We had no other issues about my son.

Over the years, I have had to fight hard for my son. Oftentimes, the very people whose job it is to teach and advocate for special needs students are the absolute worst possible individuals there are. Some of them are incompetent, lazy folks with bad attitudes, who feel that children with special needs won't amount to much anyway. There are exceptions to this rule, but they are rare.

Chapter Three

Above And Beyond

6/20/2011

I couldn't talk much when we met.

Yet you were always a comfort when I would fret. Your hugs and kisses were genuine, they let me know that I was fine.
My mom away from home you were to me.

You even changed my diaper when I did pee. Above and beyond you went for me, a blessing from God when I was three.
I'm going to miss your pretty, smiling face.

But I know you're happy to exit the rat race. Please stay in touch and never forget, the fun we had when we first met.

I wrote this poem for a teacher's aide my son had between ages three and five. She retired in 2011 and I wanted her to know how appreciative I'd been for the love she demonstrated toward my son and to all the children. I inserted a picture of her holding my son at his preschool graduation above the poem, framed it, and presented it to her in a faculty meeting at the end of the schoolyear.

Chayil learned how to read when he was six years old, just like all his peers. I burst into tears when he brought home the booklet the class had made and began reading it to me. I loved his first-grade teacher. She is the best he ever had! I was so happy that my son was reading! He *can* learn! *He's going to be okay*, I thought. Unfortunately, he would encounter a series of bad teachers who did not take him any further in his reading than his first-grade teacher had.

I asked his second-grade teacher if I could take the book home that they were reading in class, over the weekend.

"I don't give books to parents because they don't bring them back."

"I am not just a parent; I am your colleague. My office is just several yards away from your classroom door, and I don't have a problem returning your book!" She reluctantly handed it to me. Later, I confronted her about writing *very sloppy* across the top of the many dittos my son completed. After all, he was seeing an occupational therapist for motor skill issues. They removed her from that class after that year and made her a resource teacher. I wasn't the only parent who complained about her.

"Chayil had a good day today except for the student who bothered him all day." This was a note his third-grade teacher wrote to me.

"Why did you let this boy bother my son all day?" I asked.

"What? Huh?" was her response.

This woman was so nasty to my son, he developed a serious stutter by the end of the year.
His arms flailed, his eyes batted, and he stomped his foot, all in efforts to get his words out. What had she done to him? A year later in a new school district, I met my son's speech therapist. Guess what? She stuttered, too. Badly. *Was I being punked?*

I had been semi-transferred during my son's third-grade year. I was holding down my position as math coach/specialist at the elementary school, but most of my day each day, was spent teaching three algebra classes at the high school up the street. Two positions for the price of one. This teacher my son had, and my daughter's teacher for that matter, held the notion that "while the cat's away, the mice will play." Years later, my son told me that she yelled at him and his classmates all the time. She treated them as if they were despicable to her. She was a poor teacher who had borrowed tests that were given to the regular ed students, to give to my son without modifications, to justify his learning disabilities at IEP meeting time. That was her first year as a teacher. She was fired two years later. She should never have been hired.

My son started fourth grade in a different school district. I had to move to get my children away from the hateful women I worked with, who were hell-bent on mistreating my children. The special ed department was no better in the new district. His fourth-grade teacher pushed a stack of dittos under my nose during a parent teacher conference to convince me that he was too slow to be in her self-contained class.

"He doesn't even know how to spell his last name correctly," the teacher said.

"That's strange because he knew how to spell his last name before he entered your class. Why didn't you correct him the *first* time he misspelled his name? Why did you let him misspell his name so many times?" I asked.

She couldn't snatch those papers away from me fast enough. I went to mediation with the state against the school district after they tried to put him in a class with a dog for fifth grade. If the dog couldn't teach my son to read, write, and do arithmetic, I wanted no parts of it. Besides, he is allergic to cat and dog hair. They removed this woman from the class the following year and replaced her with a pregnant teacher who was trained in the reading program that was used to teach him to read four years prior. The fourth-grade teacher had had no training and she gave my son to her aide to be instructed by daily. His fifth-grade teacher went out on maternity leave in November, and never returned that year. He'd had a substitute the rest of the year. Ugh!

Middle school was the devil! I was up at his school so much, you would have thought I worked there. From bullies to inept teachers with bad attitudes, to unconcerned principals, I dealt with them all. After I complained to my son's sixth-grade teacher about a couple students in her class who were bullying my son, she punished my son almost daily with lunch detention for saying, "shut up" after a kid called him a mother*****, or another kicked him. The other children always got sent to another teacher's room to cool off, while my son got lunch detention. *What?*

"We don't tell people to shut up," the teacher said.

"But it's okay for students to yell profanity?" Instead of doing her job by punishing the culprits and ending the bullying, she chose to let the perps go free, and punish my son—the victim. I spent the day before the last day of school in June in my son's class all day and darn it if she didn't tell her aide to take my son to detention at lunch time. I told her my son was going with me for lunch. After lunch, I had him clean out his desk and told her he would not be returning.

His seventh-grade teacher clomped around in her four-inch heels doing absolutely nothing. When I'd found out before the start of the school year that she would be his teacher, I was hopeful. She, unlike any of his past teachers shared our ethnicity, and she was a member of my church. Surely, *she* would care. Nope.

I'd gotten weary of coming up to parent-teacher conferences, listening to her say a bunch of nothing, with her hands folded and no portfolio of work that he'd completed. Nothing had come home, so surely she had kept it to show me at conference time. Where is his classwork? What are you teaching? Where is his homework? I requested a meeting with the principal.

The principal and I had gone to the same high school. A home girl! When I'd complained to her about this teacher, she'd recommended a meeting. Do you know the teacher came to *that* meeting empty-handed, too? Oh, she wasn't *completely* empty-handed. She had a piece of paper with math websites on it that she promptly handed to me. *To me!* A math teacher/coach/specialist. She knew I was a math teacher because she'd been a student at the high school while I taught there. She and her principal were members of the same sorority. Things didn't change.

Before she went out on maternity leave in the spring, she had my son clean out his desk and bring all his work up to her. He said she threw everything in the trash knowing that she was supposed to send his work home. She and her boyfriend would always sit near us in church during the year she was my son's teacher. I'd rarely seen her in church before then. Now I see her all the time. After she gave birth, they sat right behind us one Sunday with their newborn. I didn't speak or acknowledge her at all (James 4:7). This game she was playing was going to end that day. Sure enough, after that Sunday, she found somewhere else to sit. Have not seen her since. Church folk can be messy. But "be not deceived … whatsoever a man sows that shall he also reap" (Galatians 6:7). She has a son. She will get it back.

During eighth grade, they clumped every student with an IEP into the same classes. Terrible situation for my son. The curriculum was way above his head. In February of that year, I got his placement changed. It was the best thing I could've done. The self-contained class was perfect for my son. The teacher was awesome!

My son played soccer during this year. I noticed that when he ran, his arm hung limp by his side. Same thing when he walked. This alarmed me, so I made an appointment with a neurologist who specialized in child spectrum disorders. They did a battery of tests, and in addition to mild mental retardation and ADHD, which I was already aware of, he had mild cerebral palsy. This news was horrifying to me. I was trusting God to deliver my son from the snares of his disability, and now he had a new one? *Lord, where are you? Don't you care?*

His first day in ninth grade found him at a ginormous high school with a schedule that had only four periods on it, when the day consisted of eight. Ugh! His schedule would change four times by Thanksgiving before they stuck him and his classmates in the modular building behind the main building. They had changed his placement at the end of eighth grade because they didn't want to put a teacher in the self-contained room to accommodate the students whose IEP's indicated self-contained was warranted. Well, now they had to change it back. I fussed all too loudly.

He was only with his peers at lunch time and at gym, where he sat on the bleachers all period because there were about eighty students and only two teachers. There was no assisted physical education course for special needs students in this school. Seventy five percent of his day was spent in a dusty, old building with four or five other students with severe disabilities and behavior problems. It was like a prison and did not comply with IDEA (Individuals with Disabilities and Education Act) guidelines. A babysitting service is all it amounted to, and not a particularly good one. He was regressing.

In tenth grade, my son's case manager told me that they were not going to do the series of tests that, by law, must be done every three years – a triennial review.

"Yes, you are!"

"No, we're not!"

"Yes, you are!" She and I actually went back and forth like that. I couldn't believe the belligerence of these people who couldn't be more wrong than two left feet! I hired an advocate from North Jersey. Two hours away. She came highly recommended, with a high price to match. She was worth every penny! During the initial meeting, which included the supervisor of special services, this stupid case manager kept mispronouncing my son's two-syllable name. I corrected her. She continued to mispronounce his name. When it was the speech therapist's turn to speak, she mispronounced his name, too. I corrected her. She ignored me just like her colleague had. If it hadn't been for the paid advocate who'd briefed me before the meeting, which was simply, for me to be silent, and to let her do all of the talking, I probably would have told them,

Shut up! I don't want to hear anything you have to say if you won't pronounce my son's name correctly. I remained silent.

We got what we wanted, and more. When the case manager called me days later to schedule our next meeting, she again referenced a "Khalil."

"Why do you keeping mispronouncing my son's name?" I asked.

"I know his name...Chayil..." She never mispronounced his name again.

At the next meeting, I sat across from the school's principal. The school board's *lawyer* sat at the head of this large boardroom table. Wow. There must have been twenty people in this meeting. The largest meeting I'd ever attended about my son, and with their lawyer. What were they trying to hide? My advocate had placed some fear into these folks. They realized we weren't here to play.

The meeting was audio taped. Everyone reported out what I had already read from the data they had collected and sent to me. My son had regressed. He was worse at sixteen than he'd been at thirteen. All the testing showed a regression — socially, intellectually, psychologically, physically, etc. If I were not so angry, I'd have burst into tears.

They mocked my son's desire to become an actor. I told them about one of the best in the business. James Earl Jones, who also has a speech impediment, but nonetheless was Darth Vader in the *Star Wars* franchise, and the voice of Mufasa in *The Lion King*, among his many other characters of stage and screen. I complained that my son's teacher who taught him English and Social Studies reported during the meeting that my son read on a *primary* level; but when I insisted on homework, he sent home a *tenth-grade* textbook for my son to read and find answers to the questions on the sheet he'd sent home.

"What sense did that make?" I asked the group. "Where is the curriculum to match the level that your tests indicate my son is on?" I told them that I want my son out of this school. "You have failed him! I want him in a Life Skills program, *not* a Life Skills class where models are used!"

The principal chimed in at one point exclaiming that they were getting a bed to jump start their Life Skills program next year. *What!*

My advocate said to me after the meeting, "Can you believe that %*&#@ idiot? A bed?"

"I want my son to go to (name concealed) High School. They have a Life Skills program!"

"Get a team to go and check out the school," the lawyer responded quickly. "There's another school closer to you, Mrs. Fowler with a life skills program … set it up so she can go to both and see which one she likes best." Look at Jesus! That lawyer wanted us up out of there and quick! And so did I. Quicker!

The following September found my son as a student at the school I'd advocated for him to go to during his junior year. Everything was blissful. He went on trips regularly, and he was finally in a school play that November. Not a speaking part, but he wore a costume, and was in a few scenes. His teachers were nice, and he was adjusting well. He had been petrified to go to this new school, but I assured him that it was best. Change is ten times more difficult for children and teens with disabilities. The Special Ed department ran like a well-oiled machine, until December.

There was a freshman boy in my son's class, an Italian with down syndrome who consistently called him and the other black boys in the class "niggers." My son knew that this word, angrily hurled at him by this racist classmate was insulting. I told him to talk to his case manager (also Italian) about it. HIB (Harassment, Intimidation, and Bullying, NJ law *N.J.A.C.* 6A:16-7.7) laws were implemented in schools for cases just like this. I didn't want to file a HIB yet; I was trying to give the school the opportunity to handle things.

One day, as my son was talking to his friends about his favorite performer, Chris Brown, this boy called my son a

"Chris Brown nigger!" When my son told his case manager, her response was, "Don't *you* do anything, or *you'll* get in trouble." *What?* Because the school turned a blind eye and a deaf ear to what this boy was doing, his behavior worsened.

One day as my son was sitting in class listening to his teacher teach the lesson, this disturbed boy got up out of his seat, walked across the room, picked up my son's pencil and broke it in two pieces.

"This is gonna be you!" The boy said to my son. My son stood up.

"Oh yeah, what you gonna do?" My son said.

"What you gonna do, nigger?" The boy said before spitting in my son's face.

Well, I couldn't get up to that school fast enough the very next morning. I went right into the building after waiting several minutes outside with students and staff for a fire drill, and pressed charges with one of the in-house police officers. He had two counts against him, the police officer informed me. After an investigation, I would be contacted about a court date. I contacted the principal via email, requesting a HIB be filed as well. Before I left the school, I spoke with his case manager about removing this boy from my son's class. I let her know that I had pressed charges. She did not seem happy about that at all. When I asked to speak to her supervisor, the

Director of Special Services, she went in the opposite direction of her office (I didn't know that then but realized it later) and told me she wasn't available.

"Please ask her to call me," I said and left. Four hours later when I hadn't heard from the director, I sent her an email about the situation. She called me soon afterwards. She was not apologetic but wanted me to sympathize with this boy and his parents, who "were very upset." His disability had nothing to do with his behavior I felt. It was poor parenting.

Foolishness is bound in the heart of a child; but the rod of correction shall drive it far from him. Proverbs 22:15 KJV *He that spareth his rod hateth his son: but he that loveth him chasteneth him betimes.*
Proverbs 13:24 KJV

My son may not have worn his disability on his face, but they shared the same low IQ. That's why they were classmates. Why should my son spend the year being called a nigger? And spat on? In the face? In 2013? I am a child of the sixties, and I had never experienced something so hateful as that. And I never wanted either of my children to experience that either. I was furious! She said that she could not separate them, but that she would hire a one-on-one aid for this (unruly) boy.

In March, I was leaving the bowling alley where we picked up our children every Tuesday, when I heard, "Tracy! Tracy!" It was a woman I didn't recognize. I turned and headed to my car. As I was handing my son something he needed to give to his teacher back in the bowling alley, the person who was calling my name was at my back.

"Hi Tracy, I am Frankie's (not his real name) mother." Is she for real? It was March 11th. She probably got her court letter in the mail that day and came up here to see who I was. They were never there before whenever I came to pick up my son. All four of them were standing there. Her, her two sons, and her husband. What for? Four months had passed since the incident, and I had never heard a peep from them. They must've been scared.

Their son was found guilty of a HIB infraction and now he was facing serious charges. I was infuriated. She didn't even have the decency or common courtesy to call me Mrs. Fowler. She called me Tracy, like we were ole pals or something. I turned away from them and got into my car without a word. "Process of elimination," I heard her say as they walked away.

Because the accused was a minor with a disability, the court decided to have us meet with a mediator, at a designated place in the community. Frankie's parents wrote a letter insisting his innocence, and basically blowing us off. A second meeting was set for April at the school, with a court-appointed mediator. When I showed up, I was met by this ignorant woman again.

"Tracy, we're all in the office board room."

Once inside, however, whenever she referred to me, I was "Mrs. Fowler." Seated around this large table was the mediator, who sat at the head of the table. To her left was a friend of Frankie's mother, Frankie, his mother, Frankie's behavioral specialist, who was hired that month after another parent complained about Frankie's ill behavior towards her daughter. She was seated at the opposite end of the mediator. Next was Frankie's guidance counselor, my son, me, and the freshman vice principal, who was very well acquainted with Frankie, and not for good reasons. Seated in the corner because there was no more room for him, was Frankie's one on one aid.

Six people had showed up to this meeting all to support, or who had been hired to assist this young man with severe behavioral issues. I was the only one there to speak for my son. The mediator facilitated this meeting. I explained the situation that had brought us to the meeting. I discussed incidents that my son shared with me that I had documented since I pressed charges. Everyone commented or asked questions. Frankie had been advised since the December incident, to not call anyone, least of all, Chayil, a nigger, but he had other issues that called for much needed discipline as well. His mother stated that she felt discipline was "reactionary," and when the mediator said he was facing up to two years in juvenile, she yelled across the table at me. "Is that what you want for my son? Is that what you want?" For a split second, I felt her pain. For a split second.

The rod and reproof give wisdom: but a child left to himself bringeth his mother to shame… Correct thy son, and he shall give thee rest: yea he shall give delight unto thy soul.
Proverbs 29:15 KJV

Withhold not correction from the child: for if thou beatest him with the rod, he shall not die. Thou shalt beat him with the rod, and shalt deliver his soul from hell.

Proverbs 23:13-14 NIV

We went back and forth. The mediator read a note that the child study team had drafted. It basically attempted to state that because of Frankie's disability, he could not be held accountable for his actions. Recess was called so that the mediator could speak with the judge to see if this was lawful. During recess, the principal walked in. He grinned all over Frankie and his mother.

"Are you behaving yourself? The principal asked him. It was then that I realized where I knew him from.

"Did you used to go to SMB Church?" I asked.

"Yes."

"You were a walking deacon along with my husband, Jeffery Fowler. He died in 1999."

"Yes," he said. He remembered. He asked about my mother and called her by name. "How is Ms. Vikki?"

"She is fine," I responded. My mother had been his children's Sunday school teacher.

In the five years that my son attended this school, this man did nothing to help. And I asked him to. He told me no. He was not going to help. "What do you want me to do?" he'd asked in a meeting a couple years following this one, after my son's case manager and another vice principal filed a HIB against my son when he'd told an obsessive, crazy ex-girlfriend, to "stop staring at me!" Of course, my son was not found to have broken any laws with his statement.

This principal was the epitome of the title of Sam Greenlee's book, *The Spook Who Sat By The Door*. He was not a threat to the establishment, and no real help to the brown skinned students marred by double-standards and racism. I've concluded that when those who you think are the obvious choices to help you in your dilemmas, choose not to, God is up to something magnificent. El Elohim wants to get the glory for our deliverance, and He wants to make it noticeably clear to us, and to others, that He alone gets the credit!

The mediator returned, handed the child study team note back to Frankie's mother, and stated that that is not an admissible defense. More serious now, the mediator sensed that we were not seeing eye to eye. Frankie had sat still and quiet during the four-hour long meeting. Totally out of character for him. His placement between these two familiar women was very strategic. He had been told to apologize. A gesture my son and I both nixed. Too little, too late. The mediator told me that I could go because she had a contract that the mother and son had to sign. If they signed the contract, this would be the end of it. If not, I would receive notice about a court date. However, because he was a minor, I was not privy to what was in the contract and could not stay.

She did not sign the contract, and a court date was set. I paid $1500 to my lawyer to speak on behalf of my son in court, and these people did not even bother to show up! Ugh! Instead, they sent a note which the judge read. This time they got the pediatrician to state that Frankie's disability excused him of any criminal act. If that defense didn't work before, what made them think it would work now?

A second court date was set. Frankie's lawyer called me, and I gave him my lawyer's number. It was now in the prosecutor's hands. I no longer needed a lawyer. When we showed up for court, the prosecutor told me that we could not attend this hearing because it was designed to determine if Frankie was competent enough to stand trial. He passed the test, and my son and I headed back to court. It was September now, and we had to take the day off. I almost did not recognize the young man in the plaid shirt seated so angelically next to his lawyer in the first row. We were escorted to the last row.

This small court room was packed. These people were not spectators. Juvenile cases are private and sealed, so these people were lawyers, police officers, or employees of the court. I saw a woman across the room I knew from church. I almost waved to her, but I caught myself. She recognized me, but gave me a look like it wasn't appropriate for me to acknowledge her. There was another woman I went to college with. She did not appear approachable either. I had a little attitude. Oh well, I thought. They were at work and it was not time to be social.

I was told I could write a victim's statement. The judge asked me to read it. He interrupted a few times to question a comment I'd made in my document. When I finished, he said, "That was very well written." What a huge compliment coming from a judge! Someone who has listened to countless testimonies, statements, and lawyer arguments. He began to expound on the history of the word, *nigger*, and its negative connotation. He was a black man, although you couldn't tell until he spoke, because he was so fair skinned.

"That was very well written," the judge said again regarding my victim's statement. He pulled out another point I had made in my statement, expounded on it, and commented a third time that my statement was very well written. I asked if the court could send Frankie to a school for students with behavior problems because of his poor social skills. The judge laughed and said that school boards don't like to be told what to do by judges. Frankie's mother was given the opportunity to speak, and she blamed her son's use of that word on an African American student who'd graduated that June.

"Henry Johnson told my son to call Chayil that word!" Frankie's mother exclaimed.

In the end, the judge meted out his sentence, and hit his gavel. Frankie's mother grabbed him by the arm and ran out of the courtroom.

By December, I was summoned to what was called a case conference. Ever since court, the school decided to retaliate against my son. Two administrators pulled my son out of class to frisk him. He had to take his shoes off and pull out his pants pockets. The male administrator patted him down; they went through his bookbag. Apparently, they had received an "anonymous" email accusing my son of passing out "little blue pills" on the school trip. It wasn't hard to guess who that may have come from.

My son's job coaching course teachers allowed a student to verbally harass my son daily. This boy cursed my son, called him a motherf****r, among other things daily, while the teachers said nothing! The day my son cursed back, I get a phone call from the case manager, trying to convince me that my son has a behavior problem. When I asked the teacher why he never intervened when the boy would walk over to my son and curse him out for no reason, he said he was teaching them to resolve their own issues. *What?* Please miss me with the BS.

"Then why are you calling me?" I asked. "Did you call the other boy's parents?" No answer for that question.

For the first time in his life, my son was suspended after a girl walked up to him and punched him hard for no reason. He punched her back. If a female does not want to get hit by a male, then don't hit males. *Periodt!* She was suspended, too. I documented everything! Dates, times, places, people, phone calls—everything! They just kept dragging my son in and out of their offices for dumb stuff. Four administrators, along with his meddlesome case manager, converged on him to admonish him about personal space. Something all disabled individuals struggle with. The statements they wrote about my son in his IEP made him unrecognizable. They were horrible. His IEP wasn't just a document that sat in a file in the school, I had to use it to get him services outside of the school, from monetary benefits to transportation. I couldn't work with their poorly written lies about my son!

They harassed my son because this racist boy got his just due in court. Thankfully, he was not in any of my son's classes that year, my son's senior year. By November, I'd typed up my documentation and requested a meeting to discuss an end to the harassment. I'd hand-delivered a copy to his case manager and to the principal. I had them sign to indicate receipt of my document. This school was out of district, so my son had two case managers—an African American woman at the local school district, and the Italian woman at the school he actually attended.

Every time something went down, it was the African American who I spoke to over the phone. She always sided with the school, and never with my son.

"I think it's time for Chayil to go to another school since you don't like this one," she said. *Was she serious?* Totally dismissing the harassment my son was experiencing and making it about me. During this conversation, she made threats of exposing a situation my son had been involved in previously. I told her that if she was not going to do anything to end the harassment, I was going to contact the county and/or state director of Special Services. In an email, I told her, among other things, that if the other school district wasn't paying her, she was working for free. "No, we're not going anywhere," I told her. We're going to fight these demons right where we are!

On December 3rd, a year to the date that the incident happened, I was in a meeting with six of the most inept, hateful people I'd ever met. The director of Special Services, a white petite woman in her late sixties; and the white case manager represented the out of district school. The local school district where we lived was represented by the director of Special Services, a white male; and the supervisor of Special Services, a black male, and the black female case manager. Rounding out this group was a therapist I'd sent my son to for counseling, also African American. He had been a case manager at the local school district and was very familiar with everyone in attendance. And supportive of them as well. I'd paid him to come to support my son. Poor mistake on my part. Extremely poor. The elder white woman did all the talking.

"We like your son. We don't like you. And if you don't stop complaining about us, we will terminate your son's placement. I don't have to provide a safe environment for your son because he does not live in our township. My duty is to the students who live here in this township!" I angrily interjected how wrong her statement was. *How can you say that you like my son when all the hateful things you were doing was being done to him? I wasn't sitting in vice principal's offices, dragged out of math class to defend some silly accusation, time, and time again. These hateful people were doing this to my son. They didn't care that I too, was an educator. They just saw a single black woman, whatever that meant to them.*

"It is a waste of our administrators time to deal with your son and his issues. Don't call me anymore! And if you call, you call *them*! You live in their township!" She stated as she pointed to the black female case manager. "And when you call don't complain about us like you've been complaining", said the director of special services at the out of district school.

I'd heard enough. Who the h*** did she think she was talking to? She can't terminate anybody's placement immediately. I would have hit them with a Stay Put order. I began to yell above her hostile rants. The therapist yelled across the table at me.

"You be quiet or they will put your son out of here!" He said this repeatedly as I yelled back in response to her threats. What an "Uncle Tom" he was. I could not believe this circus I was witnessing. The case managers who were seated next to each other, sneered at me as if to say, "We got you now!" The other two men remained extremely quiet. I had previously told the black case manager that I wanted a different case manager. She obviously shared that with them because the white case manager sneered, "I am the only case manager there is." She and the rest of them would find out how wrong they were.

And we know that all things work together for good to them that love God, to them who are the called according to his purpose. For whom he did foreknow, he also did predestinate to be conformed to the image of his Son, that he might be the firstborn among many brethren. Moreover, whom he did predestinate, them he also called:

and whom he called, them he also justified: and whom he justified, them he also glorified. What shall we then say to these things? If God be for us, who can be against us? He that spared not his own Son, but delivered him up for us all, how shall he not with him also freely give us all things? Who shall lay anything to the charge of God's elect? It is God that justifieth. Who is he that condemneth? It is Christ that died, yea rather, that is risen again, who is even at the right hand of God, who also maketh intercession for us. Who shall separate us from the love of Christ? shall tribulation, or distress, or persecution, or famine, or nakedness, or peril, or sword? As it is written, For thy sake we are killed all the day long; we are accounted as sheep for the slaughter. Nay, in all these things we are more than conquerors through him that loved us.

Romans 8:28-37 KJV

We don't work *to* victory; we work *from* victory. Before the problem introduced itself, God had already mapped out the plan that would devastate our enemy — the devil. People are not our enemies. That fallen angel and his helpers are.

For we wrestle not against flesh and blood, but against principalities, against powers, against the rulers of the darkness of this world, against spiritual wickedness in high places.

Ephesians 6:12 KJV

No need to fuss and cuss and act a fool in front of folks. Just give it to Jesus and watch Him work. At meeting's end, I played nice. The male director from the local school district told me I should shake hands and promise, more or less, to be a nice little girl, and leave them all alone.

"You pressed charges against a boy with Down Syndrome!" The black case manager angrily announced. And there it was.

Without even knowing it, she *admitted* the very reason why she and the rest of these idiots were exacting revenge onto my son. Not only that, she in her blind hatred of me, dismissed the fact that my son was called a *nigger*, multiple times, and spat on. This should have not only outraged *her*, but also the other two African American males in the room. They were more concerned for the racist student from another school district than the student who shared their ethnicity in *their own* school district. Shame. What utter self-hatred!

Prior to this meeting, a state advocate told me to contact the Office of Civil Rights (OCR)—the feds. This "case conference" sounded suspicious to her. I told her I would give them the benefit of the doubt. Ha! They showed their hand, while mine was kept hidden. I feared for my son's safety, so I shook hands with the grand dame, smiled, and left. I had an aunt who was the director of Advocacy Services in her state. I called her when I got home, and she answered. She told me the same thing the advocate had told me and added more. Divine Intervention! I filed my complaint against both school districts.

Four months later, on April 8th, I got my letter from OCR indicating that my son indeed was a victim of harassment, and that they were going into both schools to investigate. Hallelujah! And the icing on the cake? I received a letter from the very hostile, forty-two-year veteran director of Special Services, announcing her retirement, effective April 30th! Look at Jesus! Moved that windbag completely out of the way! Nobody retires in April.

In my son's yearbook that year, there were pictures of all staff that were retiring that year. Guess who wasn't featured? This director of Special Services had not planned to retire that year. She was either forced to do so or ran scared. Either way, this was the hand of my Savior – the Lord Jesus Christ, who is in control of everything. Everything they did wrong they had to redo, and the two superintendents had to sign off on everything. The OCR mandated that there had to be training classes of special ed personnel, and they had to turn in the attendance sheets of those training sessions, the name of the presenter(s), and their credentials, forms were changed, along with procedures that fell in line with the laws under IDEA.

Yaasss! Finally, these incompetent boobs were being held accountable. Wrongs were being righted. And not just for my son, but for all special ed students in these two districts. I don't understand why they thought bullying me was the best choice to make. Your arms are too short to box with Elohim! The next act was to replace the evil case manager (from the outside district) with a much nicer, and more competent one. Some personnel had a hard time adjusting, and I had to go to the school a couple of times to set some folks straight and attend a mediation meeting with the state. But in the end, Chayil finally got what he went there to get – a top notch education and post graduate job training.

A month before my son's last day at the school, I received a letter from the OCR letting me know that they had concluded their investigation.

"It has been a pleasure, and if you ever need us again, don't hesitate to call us," they'd written in the letter. They'd spent four out of the five years my son attended that school, monitoring them. Stayed with my son until he'd completed his public-school education at the age of twenty-one. There were even some tears shed by a few of the people who had given him the most trouble. God does amazing things when we put our trust in Him! I am happy to say my son is doing well and working hard at his first paying job. *Praise the Lord!*

Many are the afflictions of the righteous: but the LORD delivereth him out of them all.

Psalm 34:19 KJV

Sugar and Spice, and Everything Nice; That's What Little Girls Are Made Of

The announcement that my husband and I were expecting our second child didn't go the way I had envisioned. My son was six months old when I realized I was pregnant again. It was too soon, I thought. The realization was bittersweet. I told my husband immediately, but told him not to tell anyone. I was three months along before I finally went to my OB/GYN. I felt that if I didn't address it, it would go away. Well, as my baby and belly grew, I had to face reality.

I was at my grandmother's house one day after work. She babysat my son at the time. My mother and my mother-in law stopped by to visit. My grandmother and son were in the kitchen, while the two grandmothers and myself chatted in the living room. What a perfect time to share the great news. "Jeffery and I are expecting our second child."

"What! Pregnant? Again? I don't want a whole bunch of grandchildren! I'm going to talk to Jeffery!" My mother-in law seemed outraged by the news. I was surprisingly calm after hearing this upsetting rejection of our unborn child.

"Talk to my husband about what?" I asked. "You don't need to talk to him about anything. We are married, and the Bible says to married couples, be fruitful and multiply. So, we can have as many children as we want."

With that, she jumped up off the couch, stormed into the kitchen where my grandmother was. Then, she huffed past us, and went out the front door. I could not believe the temper tantrum I had just witnessed. I looked over at my mother who had been extremely quiet during this exchange. She never said a word, not even after my mother-in-law left. Hmm. What was *she* thinking? So much bothered me about this hateful reaction.

She was nineteen and unmarried when she gave birth to my husband. She married his father later and had one other son. My husband's brother had two children before he and their mother married. Had she been as outraged with them? My husband and I had never even had sex with each other prior to our wedding—let alone children—and this is the response I get for sharing this awesome news? We had never lived with anyone else. We had our own house, good jobs, cars and just one other child. We were not teenagers; we were in our thirties for heaven's sake. She only had three grandchildren and one on the way. *What was she so upset about?* My son had a pair of booties from her. That's it. So, what was the problem, ma'am? Oh well, life goes on.

My pregnancy and delivery went great. No broken bones or induction. During my first trimester of pregnancy with my son, I fell and broke my ankle. The winter of 1996 was amongst the worst recorded in history. And in January of that year, I fell in the middle of the icy snow-capped street. I wore a cast that went from my toes to my knee. My principal at the time, told me that I was a liability, and that I shouldn't return to work until my cast came off. Fine with me! Hopping around on crutches while pregnant was not fun. I didn't go back to work until May that year, and my ankle was still a bit sore then.

By the time my second pregnancy rolled around, my ankle was as good as new! I'd even sponsored a few walking trips with my eighth graders, from our school to a local hospital. I wanted them to get a behind-the-scenes look at careers in medicine. Seeing fetuses in jars was very jarring for a pregnant woman, however. Pun intended. Anyhoo, carrying this second baby gave me a vitality and energy I did not experience during my first pregnancy, where I was nauseous for the first six months. I'd also developed gestational hypertension while carrying my son. I had to pee in a large plastic jug, which I took to every pre-natal appointment so my urine could be analyzed. None of that was the case this second time around.

The day I was scheduled for another induction, the labor pains hit me at six a.m. Woke me right out of a sound sleep! Boy, are those pains the worst! And the pain only intensifies as the minutes and hours go by. By the time we got to the hospital, I could barely walk. I was sobbing, yet trying to keep my composure. I didn't need an induction; Baby Fowler was coming on its own!

I was in a full-on bawl every time the pain hit me, they were getting closer and closer together. The nurse admonished me to "Breathe!" I tried, through tears and snot, doubled over. My poor husband thought he was being helpful by watching the monitor and telling me when the next pain would hit. I tried extremely hard not to curse him out. Thank God, I didn't. After my epidural, I could relax a bit. We didn't know the sex, but we had prayed for a little girl, and had already picked out a name.

I was watching Oprah on the TV in my delivery room. Holly and Rodney Peete were guests. She had just given birth to twins, and I wanted to see them. But Baby Fowler was making its entrance. A nurse ran into the room, flung open my legs and yelled, "The baby's coming!" I could not feel much below my waist, except pressure. Aww man, I am going to miss the show, I thought.

Several strangers stood at the foot of my bed, smiling and ordering me to push. My doctor was in there somewhere.

"This baby has a head full of hair!" She exclaimed. "Push! Push!" The head was out. I was spent!

"Push! Push! It's a girl!" I started to cry. But wait, why isn't my baby crying? My son was screaming his head off as his head popped out. This baby hadn't said anything. They rushed her over to a table where the pediatrician and a few others were gathered. I couldn't see her, and we still hadn't heard any sound from her. I was crying and praying. Jeff was standing with bated breath. Finally, the sound we were all waiting for. *Waaaa!*

They handed me my seven-pound, six-ounce, swaddled baby girl. She was beautiful! Did they pinch her to get her to cry? Unlike her older brother, she had no health issues, and when I left the hospital, so did she. We named our daughter Charis, which means "grace; that which affords joy, pleasure, delight, sweetness, charm, loveliness: grace of speech, good will, loving-kindness, favour." This Greek word is found throughout the New Testament as in 2 John 1:3.

My daughter would stare at me all the time. She was a quiet baby. When she was too young to sit up on her own, we had put her in the baby seat, and she would follow me with her eyes. It was almost eerie how hard she would stare at me. "That's my mommy" she would probably say if she could talk. She sucked her thumb at birth. Right in the delivery room, with her eyes closed, she sniffed out her thumb and placed it right in her mouth. She looked so cute!

That tiny thumb came in handy, because I was terribly busy right after our daughter was born. My husband's health took a turn for the worse. One of his kidneys shut down, and because I was taking care of him and our one-year-old, I could not always get to her right-away. She'd lay in bed and suck her thumb. I always knew when she was up. I could sense it and hear her. She didn't scream her head off like her brother had when he was a baby.

She was patient with me, letting me do what I needed to do before I could tend to her needs. If she had her thumb, she was okay. No longer a thumb sucker, she is very laid back, and calm. Unbothered. Makes do. Do not have it? Oh well.

"No, I don't need another pair of jeans," she would say. *Whose child is this?* I fret about everything, scream, and holler. "Mom, stop stressing." She calms me. Takes everything in stride. As I write this, we are in our fifth week of a worldwide quarantine. Her college graduation ceremony, which was scheduled for next month, has been canceled. I was more torn up about it than she was. "As long as I get my degree," she said. Sigh.

And oh, so smart she is! She was speaking in short complete sentences at one year old! Whatever Chayil struggled to do developmentally and academically, she aced. She read Spike Lee's book, *Please Baby Please* to her pre-school class when she was four. She also read to a fourth-grade class that same year during Dr. Seuss week. When her teeth began to buck because of her thumb-sucking, among other non-sanitary issues young thumb suckers experience, I took her to an orthodontist who specialized with children. He said she was too young at five, to handle the bracket that is placed in the upper part of the mouth to break the thumb-sucking habit. We returned a year later. Her thumb had a hard bump on it, and it was lighter than the rest of her fingers. She had two rows of front teeth. Never saw *that* before. I had to get my baby all the way straight! She started wearing braces in middle school. For over four years! I regret however, that the braces removed the gap between her two front teeth. It was a distinguishing, unique aspect of her pretty smile, along with her dimples, that I liked.

My daughter was smart beyond her years. The teacher who'd put my son in timeout for saying hi to me, recently stated this. She recalled the pre-school graduation ceremony where my daughter was the only child who knew all the words to the songs, and the dances. She even knew the other children's parts. I recalled that, too, and had videotaped it. But I also recalled some other things as well.

A month prior to this ceremony, during the end of the year review, I'd asked my daughter's teacher–my colleague, why she had never chosen my daughter (the brightest in the class) as student of the month. I'd noticed in years past; she'd doubled up on her monthly selections to make sure every child in her a.m. and p.m. classes were featured. I walked past the bulletin board where these children were featured, every day of every month for years, and still do; but *that* year, my daughter was never featured. This teacher even chose the worst behaved little boy in the class *twice*, as student of the month. The boy's mother threatened to beat up the principal a year later, and by the time he got to first grade, the administration had kicked him out of the school. That is how bad he (and his mother) was. But my sweet-faced child had never been highlighted.

"Why?" I had asked.

"Charis is bossy! She bosses all the other kids."

"That's 90% of all the little girls in the building." I stated. And besides, I thought, she has a wisdom that they just do not have yet. So yes, it makes sense that she has to tell them what to do and how to do it. Whatever.

In kindergarten, my daughter had a BFF whose mother was a nurse. And apparently this woman shared everything with her daughter. *Everything.* One evening, my daughter walked into my bedroom. She hopped up on my bed, spread her legs as wide as she could, and pointed between her legs.

"Mommy, Lisa said babies come from here and it hurts!" Charis stated emphatically. Well, I lost it. I rolled off the bed and onto the floor in laughter. I cracked up. I was also in shock. This was not the conversation I was ready to have with a *five-year-old*. I thought I had about eight more years before it was time to have "the talk." When I regained my composure, I slowly rose to see that she was still in the same position, face as serious as could be, patiently waiting. She wanted answers, and quick. I cracked up even more. I don't remember what I said to her that day, but whatever it was, it was enough to satisfy her curiosity and qualm her fears.

It's funny because when my children were ten and eleven, I eventually sat them down to have *the talk*. I had gone to the nurse at my school and gotten the booklets and kits that were given to the children in fifth grade about their reproductive organs. I handed this material to my children and started speaking. Before I finished my sentence, my children jumped up out of their chairs and ran out of the room in embarrassment. What in the world? That was so funny! They did not want to hear about sex from me, their mother. Over the years, I managed to sneak it in without making it a formality. They listened, and so have I. In this information age, our children know way more than they probably should, at much younger ages.

That same year, my children, my mother-in-law, and I went to Mexico for Christmas. We stayed at an all-inclusive resort in Riviera Maya. After dinner, outside of the dining hall, a young man rolled various flavored cigars. They were long and skinny. At the time, it was the thing in Hollywood. Female celebrities were featured in fashion magazines with cigars hanging from the lips of well-beat faces, and finely manicured fingers. I paid ten dollars for a strawberry flavored one.

After I put the children to bed, I drew the curtains and sat out on the balcony. I was ready to take my first-ever drag of a cigar. My uncle smoked cigars, and he made it look so easy. Nothing to it but to do it. My first two drags nearly killed me. I sucked in the smoke and swallowed it. The smoke burned my esophagus. I coughed and gagged. Tears streamed down my face. Someone walked by and asked, "Are you okay?" I waved an affirmative "OK" sign, as I was not yet able to speak.

Finally, I was able to get the wind back in my lungs. Wooo! *Okay, don't suck the smoke in, girl.* I took another puff, this time making sure I didn't take it in. Somehow, some smoke made it to the back of my throat. Again, I was choking and coughing with tears and snot, trying to catch my breath. *I am gonna get this right if it kills me! After all, I paid a whopping ten dollars for this one little cigar.* Just then, I turned around to see two pairs of little eyeballs staring at me. *Oh no! What are they doing up!* I went back inside. My cigar smoking ended that night. I threw the rest of that thing in the trash and haven't picked up another since.

Weeks later, I was at work, and an aid in my daughter's kindergarten class came up to me, cracking up. She was laughing so hard, she could barely tell me her funny story. Apparently during health class, the teacher was teaching the dangers of smoking. My daughter raised her little hand and asked, "Is my mommy gonna die?" They wanted to know why she would ask such a question.

"Because my mommy was smoking a cigar and was coughing." That little girl of mine. She put all my business in the street.

Chapter Four

I Know Love

February 2002

I know love, I heard it yesterday,
It was in the voice of my son
when he asked if he could play.
I know love, I saw it last night, It
was in the eyes of my daughter
when I told her everything's
alright.
I know love

I felt it today

When I closed my eyes
and began to pray.

Teach Your Children to Love the Skin They're in

As a teacher in a suburban school district, I often get dismayed by some African American students, and parents who have obvious, self-loathing issues. I am the only African American teacher at the school, where I've been since 2001. I am a math coach, and every classroom teacher is, and has always been white. I'm the only person in my building who holds a degree in math *and* a teaching certificate in secondary math, despite that every classroom teacher in our elementary school teaches math. I've had a few black students actually argue with me about a math concept, but never argued with their white classroom teacher.

A black parent once told me, "Don't take this the wrong way, Ms. Fowler, but the reason my daughter (nine years old) argues with you (and never with her white classroom teacher) is because you're a black woman like me." *What the hell? Why?* Black mothers are the worst parents I deal with. They would email or call my principal to complain about me over the dumbest things. This past fall, a parent came up to the school after I disciplined her daughter for running around the building when she was supposed to go to the restroom and come right back.

"You told my daughter that she never pays attention or follows directions." *Was I wrong?*

"Ma'am, your daughter ran around the building."

"I know, she was mad at you." *Well, that justifies everything.*

"Your daughter has some focusing issues, and she has two F's on the first two chapter tests," I replied.

"I know my daughter is in La-La land, and she has attention deficit disorder, but she'll get over it."

Shame. This was the beginning of the second year I would teach her daughter, and her potential ADD had worsened. I gave mom a Connor's Scale to fill out so we could get an official diagnosis. A month later when I asked if she had completed the form, she said, "No, my daughter's teachers (all white) said I don't need a Connor's list." Now I doubt she asked any of my colleagues about filling out the Connor's Scale. But either way, her unspoken message to me was that she trusted *their* judgment over mine. Most of these young mothers (married or single) enjoy *making* babies, but they don't want to do the work in *raising* them.

At the end of the schoolyear, I saw that this mother had requested a child study team evaluation for her daughter to go into special education. And this is after three months of distance learning. But she didn't want to hear it from me.

One day, when I picked up my three-year-old daughter from nursery school, she was sitting at a toy vanity with two children, brushing her hair. The problem was that her hair was braided, and they were combing it out. I fussed at the workers for not watching the children.

"Charis, why did you let those kids play in your hair?"

"I want curly hair, Mommy." By curly she meant, white girl's hair—long and silky. I wound up filling two sandwich bags with the hair that came out of my daughter's hair that day. Grrr!

When she was in kindergarten, a friend of mine pointed out that the picture she'd drawn of herself was not filled in. She had not "colored" herself. I thought that this was no big deal until a colleague of mine—a young white woman, came to me to ask my advice on how to address the same issue with the parents of a black student in her first-grade class. How coincidental! I commended her for her concern and told her to simply point it out without going into a lengthy dissertation. They were not very receptive. Offended is what they were, and she said she would never bring such a touchy subject up again. Shame. I didn't take that attitude.

My mother had always taught us to love the skin we were in. Never wanted to be anything different. As a child, I'd wanted long flowing locks like the white women I'd seen in the shampoo commercials. My sister and I would tie our sweaters around our heads and pretend it was our hair. We would sling it all around until it felt like my head was gonna fall off my neck. Other than that, my reddish-brown melanin was fine with me.

As time went on, my children were moving further away from their Afrocentric roots. The TV shows were inundated with white characters and cartoons. My children watched the Disney Channel, Nickelodeon, Cartoon Network, etc. The only African American children shows were *That's So Raven* and *The Proud Family*, and they watched both. And even those shows perpetuated colorism biases that my daughter recently pointed out. I had to do something, but I didn't know what.

It's okay to embrace other cultures, but not okay to do so while hating your own. Michael Jackson was the only black person who'd semi-successfully changed his race. My children were going to love who God had made them, despite the subtle, and overt racism they experienced in school, and in all other realms of society.

We were on vacation at Universal Studios the summer following my daughter's kindergarten year. We were having a blast! I'll never forget this day. My son was holding my right hand, and my daughter was holding my left hand. She had on a white short sleeved shirt, blue denim shorts, and a white visor to keep the sun out of her eyes. As we walked the park, she looked up at me and said very solemnly, "Mommy, the kids at school call me a chocolate bar."

"What!" I yelled. "A chocolate bar? Well, you should call them—" and I thought for a minute. *Tracy girl, we are talking about five-year-olds. Their vocabulary is extremely limited. Calm yourself down.* After all, she *was* a brown-skinned girl. The only brown girl in a class full of Caucasian children. So, I smiled at my sweet-faced child, and said, "You *are* a chocolate bar. Brown and sweet, that you are!" The worrisome look on her face turned to relief and she never brought it up again. But I was still concerned.

Days after we returned from our vacation, I was seated under the hairdryer at the salon when this poem just poured out of me.

Charis

8/28/04

Hey little girl with pretty skin so brown
Why you wearin' that big ole frown?
Is it cause your hips too roun'?

Your hair so thick it won't lay down?
The pale kids at school call you a chocolate
bar, ahhh, sugary sweet, yes that you are.
Stop feelin' low 'bout who God made you
you're beautiful, and they see it, too.

You come from a long line of warriors and
queens so fierce, so fine so don't sit and whine.
Your skin is brown so you'd stand out
amongst those kids who have to shout.
"Hey look at that brown girl brown!"
"With hair so thick it won't lay down."
Hair so thick and full of life, it don't need a
daily shampoo to keep back lice.
You are beautiful from head to toe.
Strut your stuff girl, go on and show,
the world that you are proud of you.
They won't admit it but they love you too.

You are fearfully and wonderfully made.

Girls like you will never fade.

Do your thing, be who you are.

YOU ARE A PRINCESS, my little star!!!

Love,

Mommy

    I printed this, framed it, and hung it on her bedroom wall so she would see it when she needed a reminder. It worked!

No more identity problems. Nowadays, we see more and more positive images of ourselves, which is great! Just as my daughter was coming of age, we had YouTube videos that provided tutorials on how to manage our thick, voluminous type four hair. The haircare industry has boomed in the last fifteen years, to include more entrepreneurial women of color selling more organic products that do not rob our hair of its natural moisture and authenticity.

Black Girls Rock! is an annual award show that celebrates the uniqueness of our style and culture. Something that has always been lacking in this country. I taught both of my children to not gauge their self-love by how others feel about them. Love yourself despite what negativity may come your way, and always demand respect!

And give it as well.

By the time my daughter reached third grade, I put her in private school. Her second-grade teacher was the teacher from hell. She dittoed them to death, and my daughter would quickly complete her work and start a conversation with the child next to her. She was punished with recess detention excessively, unbeknownst to me. Her teacher would tell me not to come to parent-teacher conferences.

"Everything is fine. Charis is doing great," Her teacher would say. I would go anyway just to see her squirm. One day, I asked her about an F my daughter got on a quiz. "Finally, something got her goat!" She said emphatically. What a nasty, racist old woman.

Five months into the school year, I found out about my daughter's detentions behind a divider in the corner of her teacher's room during recess. When she was allowed to go outside, she had to stand against a brick wall while her classmates played. This woman hated and resented me and took it out on my sweet child. My child was never a discipline problem. She was the kind of child who'd rush to pick up whatever the teacher dropped onto the floor. She'd move chairs and tables if need be. Whatever was asked of her, she did it — no questions asked.

My daughter loved reading books. Every summer, she complained that she couldn't wait to be back in school. She loved school. This woman hated that my daughter's intelligence challenged her 1800's style of teaching. Hands folded, sitting quietly all day, while she gave her boring lectures. You don't lecture seven and eight-year-old kids. They are visual and tactile learners. I blew that woman's hair back with my letter I wrote to her about her nasty behavior against my daughter, while keeping it a secret because she knew she was wrong. I demanded a meeting with the principal. She showed up to the meeting with a union rep. I showed up with the Holy Spirit.

"I thought we were friends," she had the nerve to say. Really? What would make her think we were *friends*? What *friend* would severely punish their "friend's" child for talking in class, after finishing all their work? The principal did most of my talking for me because she knew how livid I was. The meeting ended with my demand for my daughter to never again serve another detention, and to never stand against a brick wall outside. If she finds it so difficult to communicate with me — her colleague, then don't punish my child for anything! Find some enrichment activities for her when she has completed her work.

This woman thought that because most of my day was spent down the street teaching at the high school, she could get away with her mess. That year, I held my position as math coach at the elementary school, and as an algebra teacher at the high school. She had the audacity to walk around to my office at the end of the year, to ask me if I was going to attend the baby shower of a coworker; but she'd never walked around to my office to talk to me about my daughter. No!

The Lord uses bad people and bad situations to move us into where He has destined us to be. Shortly after the meeting with the principal, I got another invitation to an open house at Friends School, a private Quaker school. I had been getting these invitations since I was pregnant with my son but had nixed them. This was divine intervention, warming me up to the idea of private school. I was a diehard public-school teacher, you see. That is, until we visited the school, and my daughter fell in love. So, did I.

I signed her up; she was tested and accepted. I paid the tuition deposit and never looked back on public education for my daughter. The teachers at Friends School did not have the narrowminded hang-ups that some of my colleagues had. They were smart and energetic. My daughter went on more school trips in third grade than she had gone on in kindergarten through second grade combined. From sixth grade through eighth grade, they went on overnight trips. She made all A's and B's each year except for the one C she got in eighth grade English. She graduated from there in eighth grade.

The next year, I sent her to a prominent Catholic high school. She was a second honors student all four years. This means that she made all A's and B's, nothing less. She was inducted into the French Honor Society and into the National Honor Society. All three colleges she applied to gave her partial scholarships, including Drexel University, to study biology. She didn't go to Drexel; she had her heart set on Fairleigh Dickenson University (FDU), where she made the Dean's List a few times as a biology major.

It was no coincidence that her second grade teacher retired the same year my daughter graduated from high school. I had to work with that woman and her resentment of me for nine more years after my daughter was in her class. Not that I ever lost any sleep about it, by the way. They passed around a composition book for everyone to write some parting words to her. This wasn't the norm. But it was divinely ordained. When the book got to me, I glued a picture of my daughter posing behind the Drexel University selfie square that read, "I got in!" The picture I copied was as large as the page. I made sure to glue it to the back of the previous sentiment. She would have to do a lot to get rid of my daughter's picture. And even if she did, she saw it. Can't erase a memory. On the facing page, I wrote some kind words, and glued another picture of my child posing in her cap and gown next to a large banner I had made, announcing her graduation, and honor student status. I never mentioned my daughter's name. She knew who she was. A picture speaks a thousand words, and I wanted this miserable woman to fully understand the message I was sending: One monkey don't stop no show!

My daughter's college graduation ceremony did not take place in 2020 due to the pandemic. There was a virtual ceremony online. The college sent her cap and gown, and we took pictures on her campus the day we were allowed back to get all her belongings out of her dorm room. The delay did not hinder her from getting a job as a lab technician working with viruses. FDU called the 2020 graduates back in May of 2021 for the formal ceremony. Thank you, Yah!

My, How You've Grown

9/2005

My how you've grown, from a
soft mushy ball, to two well-
built youngsters, sun kissed
and all. I can't wait to see you
when your growing is through.
Though I know you'll be
blessed in whatever you do!

Chapter Five

Hater

10/2007

*For years and years I cried and
cried internalizing your hate-
filled lies
"You're triflin'," "You're stupid,"*

*"You're lazy, and dumb." Your beast-like
manner has made me numb.
A mother, a nurturer you're supposed to be, but
all you've ever done was hate on me. You made
so many mistakes of your own,
pregnant with twins before you was grown.
Married a man twice that you never loved at
all, Yet always criticizing me?
What gall!*

*A mother, a nurturer you're supposed to be
but all you've ever done was hate on me.
Growing up without love is a painful thing.*

But Jeffery had much love to bring.

He showed me God's favor by making me his wife.

But you kept meddlin' and bringing the strife.

You couldn't stand to see me in love,

You wanted me beneath, and not above.
All the struggles you yourself went
through, but no one caused your mess but
you. A mother, a nurturer you're supposed
to be, but all you've ever done is hate on me.
I moved in with you while awaiting a dream
come true.

But you were hell-bent on making me blue.

Controlling, nasty, and down-right mean.

Your actions paralleled a schizo-fean.

Screamin' and hollerin' 'til you started a fight.

I'd never been as angry with you as I was that night.

Your rage and hate reverberate in my head.

You fought me as if you wanted me dead.

I'll never forget your angry
words, "Get your shit and get
out!" is what we all heard
Hugs and kisses came after I moved out.

"You're so damned phony!" I want to shout.
Sittin' in church every single Sunday, and
demon possessed all over again on Monday.
I am now at peace with you, realizing a
relationship with you I cannot do.
I'll keep my distance and constantly pray,
that you too, find peace along the way.
A mother, a nurturer you're supposed to be,
release your self-hatred, give it to Jesus, and
stop hating on me.

I wrote this poem about my mother less than a year after I'd moved into my new home. I'd been emotionally traumatized by her hate and demonic spirit during the five months I'd stayed with her while my house was being built. Her hate for me, my husband and children were unbearable at times. I loved her more than anybody has ever loved their mother. I just couldn't understand why she seemed to get joy out of inflicting pain, both physical and emotional.

To understand my mother, you must understand spiritual warfare.

For we wrestle not against flesh and blood, but against principalities, against powers, against the rulers of the darkness of this world, against spiritual wickedness in high places.
Ephesians 6:12 KJV

I kept seeing my mother as the flesh and blood person she was. The person I loved *unconditionally*. A mother is supposed to naturally love her children *unconditionally*. But that demon inside of her was irrational and hell-bent on destroying everyone around it, especially those of us who were/are Christians. She was a churchgoer, retreat attender, tithe payer, ministry member and Bible study participant. But she had no power.

"For men shall be

- lovers of their own selves,
- covetous,
- boasters,
- proud,
- blasphemers,

- disobedient to parents,
- unthankful,
- unholy,
- *Without natural affection,*
- trucebreakers,
- false accusers,
- incontinent (lacking self-restraint; not being under control)
- fierce,
- despisers of those that are good,
- traitors,
- heady,
- highminded,
- lovers of pleasures more than lovers of God;

Having a form of godliness, but denying the power thereof: from such turn away.

2 Timothy 3:2-5 KJV

My mother embodied all these traits. She was evil! Once I fully understood Ephesians 6:12 as it pertains to the unsaved, and even the saved, I knew this was spiritual warfare which could only be fought on my knees. The tears stopped flowing, the fear dissipated, and my peace began to be restored. I was dealing with a *demon,* not a mother.

For the weapons of our warfare are not carnal, but mighty through God to the pulling down of strong holds.

2 Corinthians 10:4 KJV

On June 30, 2017, the day after my birthday, my mother summoned me to her house to try to convince me that she wanted her family restored, and the only way to do so was that all five of her grown children had to meet at her house for "prayer." Prayer that she dictated and controlled. I had stopped speaking to my mother four years prior. And in the ten years since her husband's death, she had not had one occasion for all of us to meet at her house for fellowship and fun, like normal families. Not once. In *ten years.*

Her husband had cooked at all the barbeques. He had cleaned the in-ground pool each summer so we all could congregate and have fun. He cooked every Thanksgiving meal. All the while, my mother complained. All while he was doing the work, she criticized. But he did it anyway, and when the day came, guess who was front and center bossing everybody around? Yup, my mother.

A year prior, I had called her out of the blue to check in with her. During this conversation, I asked her why she had not had all of us over for fellowship in the nine years since her husband's death.

"Have you had everybody at your house for fellowship?" She quipped. I told her I had, but I wanted to know about *her*. So I asked the question again. This time she responded with, "I don't want to do all that cooking!" I reminded her that my sister and I could cook, and I assumed that my brothers' wives could cook. I'd hired a caterer for two events at her house in the past. So why was she trippin' about cooking? I asked the question a third time.

"Y'all can come over whenever you want to," she responded.

"No," I said, "I'm talking about a day when everybody is available and able to be there *together*."

She began to talk about my brothers' schedule. I cut her off by telling her that she didn't have to come up with a date at that moment. Now, a year later, I wanted no parts of this charade as she had already recused herself as the sole reason our family was in shambles.

"You're supposed to be a deaconess and you don't even speak to your brothers!" she'd angrily hurled at me at the beginning of our conversation. "The Bible says that if you have ought with your brother, to leave your prayer at the alter and fix that thing between you and your brother!" (Matthew 5:23, 24)

Is she for real? I thought.

"And we ain't talking about *old* stuff," she went on. "Forgetting those things which are behind, and reaching forth unto those things ..." She had started quoting Philippians 3:13b. Oh my God. When she asked how we can get the family back together and paused, I knew it was my turn to speak.

"Well," I began, "when a doctor finds cancer in a patient, he doesn't say, 'you have cancer, but just go on your way, and maybe it will heal on its own.' He tries various methods." And before I could finish my eloquent analogy, she retorted, "What do you want to talk about then?"

"Do you speak to your brother? Or to your sister for that matter?" I asked. A year prior, my mother stood over her older sister's hospital bed screaming at her publicly, because my aunt didn't give the house my grandmother left to her, to my brother. My mother accused her of being a crack addict and had even called me with that lie among others. She was spreading that horrible lie throughout our family. The devil kicks you when you are down. My then seventy-five-year-old aunt had been hit by a car and had suffered a concussion. When I visited her, her face was swollen, black and bruised. They wound up putting a metal rod in her leg to keep it together.

I asked my mother if her sister had ever screamed at her about the *two* houses her mother had given to her. She looked at me as if she had just lost a bet. No answer. If my mother's appalling antics at the hospital weren't bad enough, months later, after my aunt was finally able to go back home, my mother went to her house and berated her some more! She had the nerve to try to justify her terrible behavior while sitting in her dining room, but I wouldn't let her. I found out later that she went to her sister's house the day after our conversation and apologized to her. A whole year after screaming at her about an issue that had nothing at all to do with my mother. But that was her. Always in everybody's business, telling them what to do, and how to do it.

Think not that I am come to send peace on earth: I came not to send peace, but a sword. For I am come to set a man at variance against his father, and the daughter against her mother, and the daughter in law against her mother-in-law. And a man's foes shall be they of his own household. He that loveth father or mother more than me is not worthy of me: and he that loveth son or daughter more than me is not worthy of me.

Matthew 10:34-37 KJV

I had stopped speaking to my mother in July of 2013. Whenever I did see her afterwards, at a funeral, or wedding of a relative, she would roll her eyes and turn her back towards me. Just three months prior to this conversation, she turned her back to me twice, as I passed her and spoke at a funeral. When we'd made eye contact, she stuck her face out with narrowed eyes and pursed lips. I almost burst into laughter because she reminded me of the children I teach. If my mother had greeted me this day with a hug, said *Happy Belated Birthday (my birthday was the 29th, just the day before), I miss you, and want our family back together again, how do we do that?* I would have been all for it; but she wasn't ready to do the work. She wanted everyone to bury their hurt and pain, and pretend we were alright with the offenses we'd suffered, not only from her, but by one another.

My brother Harold had assaulted me twice. *In church*! The first assault was when he bent down to hug my children. When I leaned in to hug him, he pushed me away. Angrily fussing at me about giving his phone number to my half sister, who called him about a business proposition. Really? Right in front of everyone in the crowded Sunday afternoon hallway.

The second time was a few years later at church after Sunday service. We were in the crowded hallway outside of the sanctuary. He introduced me to the woman he'd been living with while he was still married. His divorce had recently become final, and they had just gotten engaged. As I peered at the engagement ring, I told her that I hoped she was not like his first wife, who'd rolled her eyes at me throughout their wedding day. Before I could finish my statement, he grabbed me and pushed me almost up against the wall, telling me that what I was saying was not appropriate.

"Everything you do is not appropriate!" I told him.

"Well, if I said or did anything inappropriate, you deserved it!" I deserved it? Really? I could not believe the hate this simpleton was exhibiting publicly. He was fourteen years younger, and thought that his six-foot, five-inch frame intimidated *me*? I had done so much for my brothers. Out of love. When I love, I love *hard*. And this brother of mine had benefited from the love that I had for him. But after my husband's death, he became a bully with serious entitlement issues, among other things.

I'd bathed and fed him when he couldn't do it for himself. Babysat him and changed his poopy diapers. When he was three, my sister and I walked him to his babysitter's house each day before we went to school. We picked him up on our way back home. When he had graduated from eighth grade, my sister and I threw him a party. Our brother James DJ'd as he and his friends danced the night away. When Harold got his driver's license at sixteen, I took him to Houlihan's for a celebratory dinner. When he went off to college, I bought him two outfits at a big and tall men's clothing store. In addition to the hefty price tag, they had to be tailored. I'd even sent him a few dollars while he attended college in Tennessee.

When my husband died, I let him borrow my car on the weekends. I used the SUV because it was bigger, but the sedan just sat in my driveway. Whenever I'd asked him to do anything for me, he always protested. But he always expected me to do whatsoever *he* asked. Nonetheless, when he'd asked if he could borrow my car each weekend, I relented. He was about twenty-three years old at the time. Each weekend, he'd bring my car back later and later. Instead of Sunday as promised, I wouldn't see him until Wednesday. Still, I couldn't get him to do anything for me—rake leaves, shovel snow, go to the store, nothing. And the only time he'd call me was to borrow my car.

So, I called him on a Friday evening before he was to pick up my car. I told him how I felt, and that he could not borrow my car anymore. He never said a word in protest. He must've had a gorgeous date lined up because he was pissed. My sister told me that my mother asked her, "What is *her* problem?" I have a problem because I don't wish to be used? I thought he'd gotten over his anger by the time he got engaged years later. He called me a month before his wedding. The first thing he said after my initial hello was, "Go buy Charis a flower girl dress. I'm getting married and we want Charis to be our flower girl." I immediately knew the game he was playing. He was about to hang up when I asked, "What are your wedding colors?"

"Lavender and white."

Well, I never wasted my time or money buying a flower girl dress. First of all, you give people more than a month's notice. Secondly, I knew he was trying to get me back for throwing a monkey wrench in his plans several years prior, by not letting him use my car. When he called a couple weeks prior to his wedding, he asked if I had bought the dress.

"Yes," I lied.

"Well, we're not having a flower girl in our wedding, and no kids are allowed at our wedding." Wow. His niece and nephew were not welcome to his wedding.

"What kind of wedding is that with no flower girl?" I asked. I don't remember his response but I'm sure it was stupid. I found a babysitter and went anyway. If I had to do it over again, I would have stayed home. His wife whom I'd only seen once, and her mother who I'd never met, rolled their eyes at me and didn't speak back to me when I spoke. What in the world? Harold rolled his eyes and was bitter towards me as well. Nothing had transpired to cause these three to act the way that they had. The last time I'd seen these two was on Mother's Day at my mother's house. We had laughed and had a good time.

I ignored their ignorance and headed for the table where my brother was seated at his reception. I was prepared to give him my wedding gift, and a few words of wisdom about marriage. When he turned to see me seated next to him, he angrily shouted, "What are *you* doing up here! You don't belong up here! Get away from here!" And with that, I put the card with money, back into my purse and walked back to my seat. If I had driven myself, and not ridden with my parents, I would have left.

About a month or so after Harold's wedding, my sister called me from a car rental place. Her credit card wouldn't go through. She asked if I could come with my credit card so Harold could rent a car to go to Tennessee. I was still in *please love me, I'm a good person* mode, when I packed my kids in the car and drove the ninety-minute highway round trip, to plop my credit card up on the counter just for him to barely say thank you, hurriedly get into the car, and speed off.

When he sent me an invitation to their baby shower a few years later, again indicating that my children were not welcomed, I threw it in the trash and did not bother going or buying a gift. He was an a**hole. Always had been. Evil, just like our mother, who was always in his ear with her hatred towards me. One Sunday in church, she tapped me on the shoulder.

"Harold is mad at you; we need to talk," she said. Instead of talking to her, I called him. He was mad because I did not give him my car—the car that he used to borrow. I was selling it and he didn't want to pay my asking price. He'd sat at my computer, looked up the blue book value, and told me that that is what I should be selling it for. I told him that if he didn't pay the asking price, then he wasn't getting my car. He asked to borrow it. "No," I said. That was that. After disrespecting me at his wedding, did he really think I would give him a car?

Where Harold was overly aggressive, Darrien was passive aggressive. I was twenty-four when he was born. My sister and I moved out when he was just three and a half months old. People thought he was *my* son because I had him so much. When he was in elementary school, I'd take him to work with me during the summer so my mother would not have to pay a babysitter. He was my road dog! Always in the car with me whenever I went somewhere.

Every birthday, I'd take him to the mall and let him pick out any pair of sneakers he wanted. He was my "poopy"! I'd taken he and my mom to the MOMA in New York to see the King Tut exhibit. In January of 1998, a few months after it opened on Broadway, I treated my brother Darrien, my husband, and stepfather to the play, *The Lion King*. My husband and stepfather shared the same January 23rd birthday, and this was my birthday gift to them both. The four of us had a great time. My mother was supposed to go, but she refused and sent my brother in her place. I had taken Darrien to see the cartoon years prior, so seeing the play was a special treat. Best play I have ever seen, by the way! Jeffery and I took Darrien to the Baltimore Harbor to the aquarium, weeks before our wedding.

Our wedding day was on his tenth birthday. He, my brothers John, and Harold were groomsmen. All three brothers sat at the head table with my husband and I, as members of the wedding party. At my reception, I put the spotlight on Darrien when I presented him with a birthday cake shaped like a football, because he played little league football, and I was his biggest fan. Next to my parents, of course. At *his* wedding, however, I was seated at table eleven. Not tables three, four, five, six, seven, eight, nine or ten. *Table eleven.* The ceremony and reception took place in the same room. My sister, my children, and I were banished to this table up against the back wall.

My mother was not speaking to either of us at the time, nor I her. You know how boys are with their mothers. When I confronted him later about where he had sat me, he reminded me that I said that I did not want to be seated anywhere near our mother. So, to be funny, they placed us so far back that we could not see anything but the backs of people's heads. I had missed him exchange his vows. Could not see a thing. My sister was so incensed that she left before the reception started. I should have left before the ceremony.

Darrien and his bride never came to our table like most couples do, thanking and greeting their guests. If I hadn't gone out on the dance floor and said hello... Before my sister left the building, she stopped to talk to relatives in the foyer. She told me that she noticed that our brother invited all his friends to take pictures with him and his bride, but had never asked her, or me for that matter, to take pictures with them. Despite Darrien's eventual apology amid many excuses, I still can't shake that my seat at a table in the back of the building was an indicator of where I sat in his heart.

I'd been to all three of my brothers' weddings, and you won't find me, or my sister in any of their wedding pictures. My children grew up without a father. I had three brothers I had done so much for out of sheer love, and not one of them filled in as a surrogate father figure/mentor to my children, especially to my son. My son needed a man to fill that void. My brother-in-law took my son to a couple of Phillies games and spent time talking with him, but my own brothers have never even taken him to the park to throw a ball. And my mother wanted to blame *me* for the dysfunction between me and my youngest two brothers? Nope. Her hate-preaching to them about me most of their lives was the culprit. I had asked Darrien weeks after this conversation with our mother, what *kind* words, if any, had she ever said to him about me. He hung his head in silence.

My mother was seventeen when she gave birth to me and my twin sister, at just seven months gestation. My sister was born first, and three minutes later, I made my appearance. We had a combined weight of seven pounds. As preemies, we lived in an incubator for a few months until we were big enough to go home. My sister still bears the scars of the tubes placed in her belly to feed her, because as the smallest between us, at three pounds, she could not suck on a bottle.

In the sixties, teenage pregnancy was not the celebrated thing it is today, so I imagine there was some guilt and shame attached to our entrance into the world. At the time of our birth, my grandmother, a registered nurse, was separated from her womanizing, alcoholic husband. She was supporting her twenty-year-old daughter, and my aunt's one year old daughter, her son (my uncle), and my mother, who is the youngest of her three children. I can only imagine that having two more babies to feed and care for was just too much for my grandmother.

My grandmother told me that she wanted my mother to complete high school, so my sister and I went into foster care. My mother had to repeat eleventh grade (she couldn't attend school while pregnant in those days), and complete twelfth grade. My sister and I celebrated our first birthday in foster care. My grandmother once told me that our foster parents were genuinely nice and that they wanted to adopt us.

"I wish they had" I said solemnly.

"You don't mean that," she would say.

After a little more than a year, my grandmother found out that her rebellious teen was playing hooky from school and doing the same things she was doing before she got pregnant. So, she told her to go and get us out of foster care, get a job and take care of us. This was the worst thing her mother could have made her do — be a mother. In 2016, my mother changed the whole story about us and foster care. Before her mother's death, I had never heard my mother say the words, "foster" and "care" in the same sentence, let alone share this story. But now, in her version of events, she was playing the victim in another attempt to destroy her mother's character.

When I was two, my mother married James Edward Brown, Jr., a twenty-one-year-old man who was enlisted in the Army. Born in Lubbock, Texas, he was living with his father in Camden when they met. This was my mother's ticket out of Camden. In my mother's own words, "I married James to get away from my mother."

We lived in Georgia on the Army base, and from there we moved to Denver, Colorado into the home of my stepfather's mother, Grandma Stella. She was so nice. My sister and I used to sit at her huge vanity table in her bedroom and imitate her putting on makeup. My mother used to brag about the time she chased Grandma Stella upstairs to beat her up — her mother-in-law, who was providing a roof over her and her daughters' heads.

Anyway, by the time we started kindergarten, we moved into our own house, a rancher, right across the street from our school, Columbine Elementary. My mother's marriage was tumultuous. They fought all the time. My sister and I would be awakened by my mother's screams.

"Go next door and tell Mrs. Bockums to call the police!" my mother would tell us. My stepfather had pulled the phone jack out of the wall so we couldn't call anyone from the house. I'd witnessed my stepdad snatch my baby brother James out of my mother's arms and throw him across the room into the crib so he could beat her. My mother was no match for her husband, but with any female, she was no slacker in the fighting department.

I remember the four of us being at the movies one night. I was probably four or five at the time. It's funny, the things you remember. Three young women around my parent's age seemed to be flirting with my stepdad. My mother told them she would meet them outside. We met them in the alley, and my stepdad told them that it was going to be a fair fight. My mother picked the one with the biggest mouth, and the most heart. Victoria wailed on that chick so bad, my stepdad had to break it up. The other two never attempted to jump in. My mother beat her something awful.

The next woman my mother fought had slapped me across the face after I grabbed her son and told him to leave my three-year-old brother alone.

"Go get Vicky!" my neighbors said. Some of them my mother had babysat years ago when she was a teenager. Now young adults, they had been playing baseball in the street, as I stood at the curb watching them play. They obviously had witnessed what had happened. My mother was getting ready for a Gil Scott Heron concert.

"Mommy this lady smacked me in my face!" With lightning speed, my mother raced up the block after putting her switchblade in her pocket and wailed on this woman who was shorter than my mom by a foot. The woman ran into the house. My mother cursed her and told her to bring her &#@% outside. She threw a hard object out the door towards my mom. My mom ducked. The whole neighborhood was out there now. The woman came out, and my mom whipped on her some more. Someone called the police, and they were both arrested. My mom spent the weekend in jail. With no shoes. They'd put my mother in handcuffs and into the police car without her shoes.

My grandmother spent the whole weekend blaming me for everything. To her, it was my fault that my mother was arrested. As if I was not traumatized enough, she fussed that I should not have responded to the woman the way that I had. The woman had gotten in my personal space, after someone went in her house and told her that I had grabbed her son. She yelled at me about putting my hands on her son.

"He has a mother!" she yelled angrily.

"I have a mother, too!" I'd retorted, and with that, she slapped my ten-year-old face.

When I was nine and a half, my stepfather abandoned us. That's when my grandmother sent the money for us to move back to Jersey from Denver, Colorado. My sister and I moved in with our grandmother. My mother and brothers moved into her childhood home around the corner. My grandmother gave my mother two houses. When the first house fell to disrepair, she moved her into the second house right next door to us. My grandmother had even bought my mother a van. She said my mother needed her own transportation in order to get her children to doctor's appointments and to the grocery store. My grandmother didn't drive. She never got her license.

My mother was on welfare with four children by this time. My brothers, James and John were born in Denver, Colorado.

I was six when James was born, and seven when John was born. They were twelve and a half months apart. When I was fourteen, she had Harold during the time when she and her ex-husband tried to reconcile. Ten years later, she gave birth to her fourth son, Darrien, four years after they remarried. Six children in all.

I met my biological father shortly after we returned to Camden, New Jersey. My sister and I were playing in the living room where my mother was having a conversation with a man seated across the room from her.

"Kacy and Tracy, James is not your father; this is your father." We looked up at him and went back to playing. I was confused and shocked. My daddy is not my daddy? This stranger is my daddy? Shortly after that abrupt introduction, our father took my sister and I to the corner store and bought us a cheese steak sub, a delicacy my mother could not afford. When we got back, he told my mother he wanted to take us to the movies. She agreed only if he took the whole family, including her. I was only ten, but I remembered not liking that idea. For some reason, I only wanted the three of us to go.

I remember that night as if it were yesterday. We went to see a movie that was way over my head. I think I fell asleep. Boring. On the walk home, my mother and father argued the whole time. He never came around again. I didn't see him again until I was in high school. A friend and I were watching some people play baseball at our high school football field. A tall man walked up with a broad grin on his face.

"Do you remember me?" he asked.

"Yes," I responded. "You're my mom's friend." His face fell. He actually rolled his eyes at me as he walked away. The look on his face was hurt and disgust all wrapped up in one. Did he really think I was going to embarrass myself in front of my girlfriend? She lived in a big, pretty house with *both* of her parents who loved her and her four siblings dearly. She dressed nice and her hair was always perfectly coiffed. I wore secondhand clothes, and I'd never had my hair professionally done.

Where had he been all these years? Why hadn't he stayed in touch? My mother never spoke of him. Ever. She never encouraged a relationship between us and our father. When he had a stroke in the late eighties, it was she who insisted we go visit him in the nursing home. Just like my mother to show an interest when you're down. But as long as you're on your feet, she couldn't stand you, and didn't want anything to do with you.

I went to see my father. When I walked into the room, there were two men in their beds, and I wasn't sure which one was him. I'd only seen him three times before in my whole life, and I was in my late twenties at that time. But he recognized me. It was in his eyes. He was completely nude. The nurse was changing his catheter and had just stepped into the bathroom inside his room. This uncaring woman didn't even have the decency to pull the curtain or close the door, but left him exposed to whomever entered. Which, to both of our dismay, happened to be me. My father could no longer speak and was partially paralyzed, but his eyes were telling me to get out, as his roommate chuckled in amusement. He had a muffled yell. I turned and ran out of the building and never returned. The next time I saw my father was at his funeral over two decades later.

My mother received her GED when I was eight and got her bachelor's degree in history when I was sixteen. My mother used to talk about being so smart in school that they wanted to skip her, but her mother wouldn't let them. My mother always believed my grandmother did not want her to pass her older brother who had been retained a couple of times. A cousin of ours, who was older than my mother confirmed to me once that my mother had been a very bright student, and that he understood why my grandmother did not agree with having her skip a grade. This may or may not have been in part, why my mother rebelled. Perhaps.

My mother was also ambidextrous. She'd started off lefthanded, but her teachers in those days, felt being left-handed was an abnormality, so they made her write with her right hand. She started her career as an income maintenance technician with the Board of Social Services during my senior year of high school. Having been the recipient of welfare, she was now one of the persons responsible for processing others through that same system.

My sister and I were model students and daughters. Daughters that would make any mother proud. We always got good grades and were the recipients of good citizenship awards throughout elementary school. In high school, we were inducted into the National Honor Society. I recently ran into a man I went to junior high school with. Had not seen him since eighth grade graduation and was shocked that he even recognized me. It was he who'd called out my name to get my attention. He even remembered my name. After he'd asked about my sister, he said, "You and your sister were very smart girls."

"Wow, praise the Lord," I said. That's the same thing another former high school classmate said two months ago about my sister and me. He even called me a nerd. I never felt I was smart but thank you!

My sister was the smartest between the two of us. She was our senior class president and a recipient of the coveted Dukes award at our school. A great honor bestowed upon a graduating female student each year. When they announced her name at the assembly, I leaped out of my seat, clapped and yelled her name in celebration. I was so proud of her! She sat on the dais at graduation and gave one of the many speeches, along with the rest of those seated with her. She went on to graduate summa cum laude from Seton Hall University. She worked as a TV producer for Channel 10 CBS in Philadelphia before becoming a teacher and eventually vice principal ten years before her retirement. As a teacher, she was chosen Teacher of the Year twice, and represented both her school and district at ceremonies at the state capitol.

My ninth-grade science teacher chose me to participate in a STEM program, PRIME, which stands for Philadelphia Introduction to Minority Engineering. The summer following tenth grade, I traveled to Widener University each day to participate in a PRIME sponsored program. We took math and science courses and had the run of the campus. The Philadelphia Eagles' training camp was at Widener. Ron Jaworski was the quarterback at the time. We ate lunch with them every day! Harold Carmichael and another player jokingly asked me and a friend, who we thought was the ugliest between them. When we didn't respond, they broke out in laughter.

"Man, you so ugly, you scared them!" Harold said.

They all were so nice and had great camaraderie. They invited us to their exhibition game with the Miami Dolphins. We had front row seats to witness an Eagles victory! The following summer, I commuted for two weeks to Villanova University for science and math courses in the PRIME program. There were one hundred students from the tri-state area, me included. The last four weeks, we spent living on campus in dorms. They broke us up into teams of five and entered us into a design competition between the twenty teams. My team came in second place!

Our design was a telecommunication system for the deaf/mute. When someone called or knocked on the door, a light flashed to let them know. I don't know how they would have talked on the phone; our design didn't include an apparatus for speaking. We were invited back in the fall to make our presentation to the engineering department personnel.

Right before graduation, I went on my first job interview. Engineer Intern at RCA in Camden, New Jersey. Each year, RCA selected up to four students from the two Camden city high schools to work there as an initiative to get more brown skinned people into the field of engineering. I was hired and made over $360 a week! That was a lot of money for this poor girl! Not only that, but they promised us our jobs for all four summers during college. And each year, we made more money than the previous year.

That first summer, we built a digital guessing game. I'd used an oscilloscope and soldering iron to build one of the boards in the game. On the last day, our parents were invited, and we all played the game. It was a lot of fun! Each year, I was assigned to work with a different engineer. From computer programming to solar panels, I was exposed to it all. I commuted to Rutgers University after my freshman year at Indiana Institute of Technology was a bust. Engineering was not my forte after all. I graduated from Rutgers with a degree in applied mathematics.

On my graduation day, my mother told me to invite my uncle who was visiting my grandmother. This was my mother's brother who had recently participated in a hate letter-writing campaign with me that she had orchestrated. Now, she wanted me to invite him to my big day. Just before we were about to leave the house. I invited him. And he rolled over on the couch with his butt facing me and farted. I felt like a fool. Fortunately, his ignorant behavior did not stifle the euphoria that I felt that day sitting there, waiting for my name to be called so I could walk up on that podium and get my sheepskin. *Haaaaayyyy!* I exclaimed. My mother was seven months pregnant. She was mean and crochety. Yelling and screaming all day long. Ugh!

I started teaching math in the fall. Nineteen years later, I was selected Teacher of the Year in 2005. At the school board ceremony, my mother asked why I'd worn a dress with so many colors in it.

"You're too big for all those colors," she said. Never said "congratulations" or "I'm proud of you." Body shaming was *her* forte. I made a mental note not to ever invite her again to any ceremony I was involved in.

During a biblical family counseling class at church in 1990, my mother leaned over and apologized for any abuse that she'd inflicted upon me and my sister as children. I immediately forgave her. And there was a lot to forgive.

My sister and I had walked into the house after school one day. When she perused our first-grade drawings, she immediately put me in a closet in one bedroom, and my sister in the closet in the other. I don't know what exactly angered her, but I do know children draw what they're experiencing. After a parent teacher conference in kindergarten the year prior, my mother got the scissors and began cutting my hair.

Apparently, my teacher told my mother that I did not play with my sister.

"You think you're cute? Won't play with your sister? Well, I'll cut off all your hair and you'll look like a boy!"

I cried and promised to play with my sister. But I was only mimicking what my mother was doing. My mother would take me on long walks and leave my sister home alone all day into the night. My sister said she'd sit by the window crying, afraid and hungry. We were only five years old. I can't imagine the terror in my sister's heart. Upon our return, my sister said she'd told my mother how hungry she was, and my mother angrily yelled at her to "Go to bed!" My sister remembered that I was sucking a lollipop. I believe this act of favoritism on my mother's part is the bane of our relationship to this day.

My mother used her fists when she beat us. She'd banged my head against the wall repeatedly. One time, she punched my sister in her nose and blood squirted everywhere. My worst beating was when she used an extension cord. I was eleven and had run all the way over to my aunt's house across town at night. I was trying to catch up with my mom who'd left the house earlier. She wouldn't have been the wiser because I caught up with her boyfriend at the corner of my aunt's street. Me and my big mouth told on myself.

"You're gonna get it when I get home." She ruined my whole visit with that threat. And she made good on it. You would have thought I was a grown man trying to break into her house the way she beat me.

"Vicki stop! You're gonna kill her!" Her boyfriend jumped up off the couch and snatched the extension cord from her hands.

Most mornings, my mother laid in bed as my sister and I got ready for school. Sometimes, she combed our hair, and sometimes she didn't. My sister and I were responsible for feeding our brothers in the morning before school, as our mother laid in the bed. We were always late for school even though we lived right across the street. On one snowy morning, as my sister and I crossed the street, something said "turn around." I turned around just in time to see our diaper clad brothers about to cross the street. Nothing on their feet, legs, arms or chest. Just a diaper, in the snow. They were following us to school. I screamed to my sister, and we ran back across the street, scooped them up and ran in the house to our mother's bedroom. I told my mother to get up because they could have been hit by a car!
Nonetheless, in 1990 at church, when she said, "I apologize," the remembrance of the always-existent bitter tone in my

mother's voice, peppered with contempt, beatings with her fists, and extension cords, were all forgiven. That was the first time I'd ever heard her apologize to us for anything. But now, twenty-seven years after that, she had asked to meet with me again after I told her that I wanted no parts of her shenanigans during the previous meeting. She would have to change! Sitting in my living room, she told me that the reason she had been such a monster to me, and my family was because of *"the way you are."*

"What does that mean?" I asked. I'd heard my sister and brothers use that term to describe me to justify their poor behavior towards me.

"That poem you wrote, about me yelling, and that boy from Chester, Kacy told me about." How did she know about my poem? I wrote that poem when I was seventeen.
I'd never shared it with her. I'd read it to my sister once, but to no one else.

"First of all," I began, "that poem wasn't about you; it was about Grandma because she is who I lived with at the time, but if the shoe fits! Secondly, my relationship with that boy from Chester was not any of Kacy's business or yours! What did my relationship have to do with you? I was living in my own apartment then. If I were a prostitute, selling my body on

Broadway and Mickle, you are supposed to still love me unconditionally!"

It's sad that she would use a relationship that began and ended in my twenties, as a justification for her abuse of me and my children. Sitting here in my living room, she looked and sounded like a crazy person. I'm in my fifties now, and she used a relationship from thirty years ago as justification for her hate?

"Dear devil (and those you use) You can't bring up my past to break me! That's what MADE ME!"
@realtalkkim

Instagram post

June 11, 2019

"When the devil reminds you of your past, remind him of his future."
@drtonyevans

Instagram post

7/31/2019

If we confess our sins, he is faithful and just to forgive us our sins, and to cleanse us from all unrighteousness.
1 John 1:9 KJV

Being confident of this very thing, that he which hath begun a good work in you will perform it until the day of Jesus Christ:
Philippians 1:6 KJV

God will get the glory out of the believer's life. He is committed to transforming our lives—the past, present, and future. And He never fails. It will all work for our good and for His Glory! God has brought me a mighty long way and has blessed me beyond what I could have ever imagined. If you can ignore all of what He has done, to reach back decades ago and hold onto foolishness, then something is wrong with you.

This dude from Chester was someone I'd fallen madly in love with when I was twenty-five. He was the worst possible person anyone could fall in love with because he was too narcissistic and self-centered to love anyone but himself. He was a womanizer. He'd broken my heart into a million pieces. By the age of thirty, my emotional ties to him had run its course.

When I was engaged to Jeffery the first time, he made the forty-one mile trek from Chester, Pennsylvania to my church every Sunday. Before my engagement, my church as he stated, was too far to come to. When I told him Jeffery and I had broken up, he stopped coming. A couple of weeks before my wedding, he called wanting to know where his invitation was. I told him he was not invited to the reception, but he could come to the church ceremony. He got mad and said he was going fishing instead.

"Have a nice life," I told him. I was certain that that was the last of him. Five months after I got married, dude walked up to me after church service. He said hello to my husband, and family (mother, stepdad, and siblings), and asked if I was pregnant.

"Yes, how do you know?" I asked.

"I saw him (Jeffery) rubbing your back."

Two months before my son's August arrival, we were at the church picnic. Mr. Chester sat with his entourage directly across from us. When we left, he was right behind us. Walked up to me as I was headed to the car and asked when I was due. Why the sudden interest? When we were together, he'd acted like he was doing me a favor. He had a harem of women. For the four years while I was married, this dude was in church *every* Sunday. Even attended other events at the church. He sat near us, so we'd see him and he'd see us. He acted like a stalker.

When my husband's death was announced at church, he disappeared again. Ten years later, he pulled up beside me as we drove on the road near my home. He blew his horn. But I couldn't see who was behind the heavily tinted glass. When he rolled the window down, I was shocked to see him in this New Jersey suburb.

"I live around here!" he said when I asked what he was doing in the area. Two weeks later, he walked up to me at Lowe's. He told me what development he lived in. It was the *same* development I lived in! He'd moved there a year after I did. Was he stalking me? I would see him a few more times, walking in the development and at the grocery store. Saw him sporadically at church, too. I wanted no parts of whatever he was up to.

A few years later, he pulled up in front of my house as I pulled into my driveway. He was married to his third wife, he said. He wasn't even fifty yet. What in the world? He's now married to his fourth wife, and she's from Camden like me. So was his second wife. I must have made a lasting impression.

I guess my mother and sister were reading more into the antics of this crazy ex, than what was there. We all attended the same church, so they saw him all the time, too. Why would she bring *him* into her craziness? Later, when I mentioned to my sister my mother's admission about her informant duties, my sister vehemently denied ever saying anything to our mother. She became enraged and yelled at me for even believing it were true. When people act like that, they are guilty. Her response was just too bizarre.

"You believe that? You believe that?" she yelled.

"Well, yeah I do!" I responded.

"Well, I guess she accomplished what she set out to do."

"What is that?" I asked.

"Destroy our relationship!" No, dear sister; you did that all by yourself. She said she didn't want to speak to me anymore, after calling me "fake." During the several months following her tirade, whenever I tried to reason with my sister, she became a victim, erratic, and combative. She canceled the therapy session I had recommended to get our relationship back on track. And blamed me for the reason why she canceled it.

"I have to trust the process," she said. You don't trust biblical counseling? From a trained Bible counselor at the church, *you* attend? She is still stuck in the childhood abuse and trauma and made me the scapegoat. I am not surprised at her behavior. She has always been treacherous towards me. My mother later admitted that she and my sister had *ongoing* conversations about me and my personal business. Wow. I was so hurt by my sister's betrayal. Sisters are supposed to be keepers of each other's secrets. But my sister has been telling my secrets for decades to her friends, relatives, and anybody who will give her the opportunity to feel like a victim. She even went to my son's school his final year there, and bad mouthed me to the very people who tried to annihilate him, as she handed them gifts.

"Your fruit will outlive the gossip they create about you. Ignore it and chase glory." www.REALTALKKIM.com

Lie, deny, or justify — that's what my sister does whenever her unsavory actions are brought up. Unlike her, I'd always been careful not to spread her business. When a former coworker showed up at my church at three different times, looking for me, she was pretending to rekindle a friendship when all along, this deceitful gossip was trying to get in my sister's business. I'd made sure I presented my sister in the best possible light. It was only after her third visit that I realized she'd only wanted information about my sister and nothing else. The extent to which nosey people will go through to get information that has nothing to do with them. Sheesh!

When people want to hold onto *your* past, while neglecting to admit and talk about their own, they are not people you want to keep close. I suspected my sister was exposing my personal business all along. Too many signs. I pray she becomes honest about her behavior and gets healed.

"Never question who GOD REMOVED. He heard their conversation when you weren't around."
@courtneyadeleye
Instagram Post
5/27/2019

"You don't have to rebuild a relationship with everyone you've forgiven. Just because you're at peace doesn't mean that they aren't still toxic."
@realtalkkim
Instagram Post
8/4/2019

"If you want to get to where God's taking you, there are some people you may have to remove from your inner circle.

You can love people and limit them at the same time. Choose your circle wisely!"

@pastorpaulsheppard

Instagram Post

7/29/2019

When I had my son, my mother and grandmother demanded that I use PET Milk and cloth diapers. "I used PET Milk with you and your sister, and look how you turned out," she'd reasoned. So, I did. Don't judge. I was a people pleaser. To my credit, I eventually replaced the PET Milk with formula. Breastfeeding did not work for me unfortunately. I wanted these two controlling women, who I'd had on a pedestal, to be pleased and proud with me. Little did I know that would never happen no matter what I did.

One evening as my grandmother changed my daughter's diaper, we noticed a tiny rash.

"Trifling! You're just trifling! Trifling Tracy, trifling Tracy!" I was mortified that my mother was singing this insulting song right in front of my husband. I found out later that my daughter actually had eczema. So did my mother.

"My wife is not trifling!" Jeffery yelled at her. "My wife loves our children! She is a very good mother, and shame on you for calling her out of her name. This is your daughter!" My mother is crazy, but she ain't that crazy. She didn't utter a sound in response. The next day, my mother called, screaming at my husband on the phone, saying that he'd dishonored her. She used Ephesians 6:2 as a basis for her hateful rant. My mother didn't think that the scriptures applied to her. The scriptures were to be hurled like a weapon at everybody else.

Her demonic behavior was justified in her mind. She was so loud, I could hear her voice from across the room. I kept telling my husband to hang up. She'd also complained to him about a measly five dollars that his mother owed her. I was so mad at him when I heard him say, "I'm sorry," that I jumped in my car and went to her house.

"How are you going to tell my husband he dishonored *you* when you dishonored *me*?" I asked. "Keep reading, because it says, 'Fathers provoke not your children to wrath' (verse 4). My husband did what he was supposed to do. Defend his wife. And he doesn't owe you an apology for that. As my mother, you shouldn't give him a reason to have to defend me." I handed her five dollars before I left, on behalf of my husband and mother-in-law.

My daughter was born on November 12th. We were at my grandmother's annual Thanksgiving dinner two weeks later. My husband and I were sitting at the dining room table before dinner, talking to my cousin and his fiancée. I was holding our newborn daughter, and our son was playing in the living room with relatives. Then, my cousin came in.

This is my mother's sister's daughter. She and my mother were very close. *Birds of a feather...* She walked past us into the kitchen without saying hello. She left the kitchen, passed by us again and stopped in the middle of the living room. And in front of a packed house, she exclaimed, "Tracy can't cook! Never could cook!" She went on and on. My husband heard her first. He laid her out so badly, that she walked out the front door and never returned that evening. My mother sat in silence with her back to me. She was probably grinning. Now, I have a daughter. There is no way I'd sit quietly while somebody debased her. No way!

By Christmas, my husband had been hospitalized and was on temporary disability. He was feeling better, so we'd decided to go to the movies, and dropped our children off at my mother's. When my daughter was born, I threw away the cloth diapers and started using Pampers. When we returned to get our children, we were greeted with, "Didn't I tell you not to use Pampers on these babies!" My mother's first words as she opened the door to let us in. We didn't respond, so she continued.

"I threw them in the trash," she said. Before she could say another word, Jeffery Bryant Fowler went off.

"What? Do you know how much Pampers cost? Why would you throw our Pampers away?" My grandmother sneered at me.

"What kind of mother are you, using Pampers on these children?"

My husband was still fussing when my mother snatched the bag of Pampers out of hiding and threw them on the couch next to my baby.

"Here they are! Just be quiet! Everybody be quiet!" But I wanted to talk. Talk about the hate these two had for me. A week or so before, my grandmother broke my heart by telling me that I was a bad mother. I cannot recall the circumstances that prompted the worst thing you could say to a new mother. I had a one-year-old, a newborn, and a husband with renal failure. I loved my children. We always got compliments from people about our babies. They were cute, clean, and healthy. But she had said it. I'll never forget it. When I told my mother what she'd said, my mother's response was, "You are." And now that these two domineering, controlling, heartless women were together, we could hash this thing out.

I may have been a lot of things, but a bad mother I was not. I was not a bad teacher, nor was I a bad wife. As I opened my mouth to speak, my mother whirled around and punched me in my face. My glasses flew off my face and across the floor. Before I knew it, I was on top of my mother, knees in her chest, smacking her in her face. My husband was pulling me off her. He and my grandmother held her back while I put the children's snowsuits on. I wrapped them up to take them outside and put them into the car. My mother was selling wolf tickets the whole time. I know she was shocked. I had been terrified of her all my life, and she took advantage of that, being the bully that she was. Well, terror had been replaced with anger. I still loved my mom, but I was furious with her now.

Two months later, my pastor was preaching a series, *Hidden Hurts of the Believer*. My mother came over and apologized. It didn't seem sincere, but I cried, and we hugged. Days later, during a phone call, my mother made a comment about my son that hurt my feelings. After I hung up, I said out loud, that I wished I didn't have a mother. My grandmother was our in-house caregiver, under the condition that I use cloth diapers. I told her she could use them while she babysat, but I would still use Pampers. She agreed. On weekends we took her home.

Unbeknownst to me, she told my mother what I'd said. On a packed-out Easter Sunday morning, when I tried to sit in the pew with my mother and sister, my mother pushed me. My infant was in my arms when she pushed me. Meanwhile, my husband was parking the car. I found somewhere else for us to sit.

By the end of April, she called for us to meet to talk. She complained that I was telling everybody about our fight. "You don't tell people my business!" She argued. I reminded her that I was a grown, thirty-five-year-old woman. That this was *my* life, and that I will tell whomever, whatever. If she didn't want people to know what she was doing, she shouldn't act the way she does. She tried to convince me that I was wrong for hitting her back. I told her that I am not a child, and that I am not going to let her pummel me.

"You should not have hit me," I said. "I have a right to speak. They are *my* children, and you don't dictate what I put on *my* children." We reconciled. I cried, and we hugged.

A week later, I decided that we would go over to my mother's for her birthday. *I know. I am a glutton for punishment. But read on.* We were so tired between our baby, toddler and careers. Jeffery had to *be* in lineup at 6:00 a.m., and I had to be signed in at work by 7:30 a.m. Jeffery worked with criminals all day, and I worked with teenagers all day. Needless to say, we were exhausted! But we trekked on over anyway.

We had no money for a gift, but it was the thought that counted. Or maybe not. Soon as we got there, my stepdad handed Jeff some money and asked him to go get *his* wife a cake, ice cream, and soda. Now, he was retired and at home all day. Why hadn't he done that? Nonetheless, we had what I thought was a great fellowship that night. A day or two later, my mother called, and I answered the phone.

"Your husband has a problem!" My mother said in the nastiest possible voice.

"What now?" I asked.

"He stole my money!"

"What?" I asked.

"He bought two lemon pies with the money James gave him," she went on. "It's on the bottom of the receipt!"

"Did you count your change? I'm pretty sure he replaced the dollar that it cost for the pies."

I thought her insanity over this foolishness was done. A couple days later, I'd come home around midnight from a school trip to New York. My husband proceeded to tell me that my mother, her Bible, and her husband came over to tell him that "We don't have people come in off the street going in our cupboards and refrigerator." This time, her Scripture of choice was Proverbs 23:10.

I felt so sorry for my husband. He was going through some major health issues and my demon-possessed mother was whining because he poured himself a glass of soda at her house, that *he* went to the store to purchase. *Really?* He used *his* gas to get the items that her husband, who was with her supporting this foolishness, should have gotten. And instead of saying, "Thank you for coming over to celebrate my birthday," she first tried to accuse him of stealing (a dollar). That didn't work; so now, he is "somebody off the street," and not her son-in-law, the father of her grandchildren. Several months prior, she implied that he was her son, when she used Ephesians 6:2 to accuse him of dishonoring her. I truly regretted that we had wasted our time going to her house to celebrate her birthday.

Months later, when she found out Jeffery was on dialysis, she called.

"I owe him an apology. I just thought he was lazy," my mother said. I didn't have the energy to fuss, so I just handed him the phone. She, my grandmother and other relatives obsessed over me and my husband, and what we were doing. Criticizing, condemning, and finding fault all the time. The whole time my husband was on disability, my grandmother kept trying to get him to do major things around the house. If he were up to doing those things, he'd been at work, and not at home with one functioning kidney!

The morning following my husband's death, my son was extremely ill. I camped outside of his pediatrician's office until it opened. He had a fever, hadn't slept, defecated, or eaten. The doctor prescribed suppositories and sent me to the lab for bloodwork. When we got home, my house began to fill with people. Co-workers, church members, relatives and friends. My husband's cold body was still in the hospital morgue, and I hadn't had time to think about anything else.

There was a knock at the door. I opened it. My mother stepped in, frowned up her nose at the crowded room, brushed past me as she pretended to care about my son.

"Where's my baby? I heard he was sick." Somebody had called her, or she had called to be nosey. Hadn't said good morning or had even given me a hug. My grief wasn't important to her. Just the day before, she had cried the loudest over my husband's deceased body in the intensive care unit. She made her way to the bathroom where we had my son in the tub, trying to bring his fever down. She ignored all the people on the way to the bathroom. A short while later, she rudely interrupted a conversation I was having.

"You need to take him to the hospital! He needs to go to CHOP!" She said in an angry tone. There was no way I was going to sit for hours in a hospital emergency room after my ordeal over the past three weeks. I regretfully handed her my insurance card and told her to take him herself. I would later get in trouble with my pediatrician for doing so. If I could do it all over again, I would've asked her to leave.

My sister, who loved to report whatever hateful things my mother said behind my back, went with her, and reported to me that she complained.

"What kind of mother is she? Won't take her son to the hospital? In there with all them nosey church people!"

Never mind that I had taken him to the doctor's early that morning, and to the lab which was difficult because my son was petrified of needles. Several hours later, when they returned, my son was still ill. This virus he had would eventually run its course.

Two months after my husband's death, my brother John was getting married. Days before the wedding, my whole family was at my grandmother's house. This was also the evening of the wedding rehearsal. My brother, Harold asked if he could drive my car to the church. I told him he could if he came right back when rehearsal was done. Around nine p.m., my parents walked through the door.

"Where's Harold with my car?" I asked.

"I told him he could take your car to the party, and I will take you home," my mother responded.

"I told him to bring my car back here. And how am I going to get in my house when my door key is on the chain with my car keys? Why couldn't they ride in David's car?"

"Because their legs are too long!" she retorted in the nastiest, most unapologetic tone. My toddlers were already asleep, and my son had to be *on* the school bus at eight the next morning. I was so mad at her! I heard my grandmother ask her why she did that.

"These babies need to be home in the bed," my grandmother said to my mother as I stomped into the kitchen. My brother didn't pull up until 11 p.m. Ugh!

This wasn't the first time my mother had given a son of hers permission to use my car without *my* permission. When I first started teaching, my parents had a custom van. I was never allowed to ride in it though.

"You can walk!" was my mother's response as to how I would get to and from work each day. It took me an hour to walk to work, and an hour to walk back home; so each day, I walked a total of two hours. The only good thing about that was it kept me slim and trim. I was cute in the face and snatched in the waist! But I was sweaty by the time I got there.

On hot and humid days, I needed a whole bath by the time I got to work. And I had to spend the day standing in front of middle schoolers.

My stepdad worked nights, so he was back home in time to take my mother to work. He could have easily dropped me off, and then taken my mother to her job. We both worked in Camden, and both had to be at work at the same time, 8:30. Quite an easy task. Nonetheless, I walked two hours a day until that November, when my sister and I moved out and moved into an apartment. The distance was a tad bit shorter if I walked the back alleys, which I did. I prayed for my safety and carried a stick for protection. The Lord was with me in those days. Surprisingly enough, I had perfect attendance that year. Never had it any year since though.

In May of my first year as a teacher, I bought myself a car. It was a three-year-old, 1984 Chevy Nova. I was so happy to have some wheels! I didn't have to walk to work anymore. Guess who plopped herself in my car every chance she got? Mm hmm. My mother. You would have thought my little Nova was hers.

One night as I was sitting in the passenger's seat of my own car, I told my mother to drop me off at home. We were closer to my apartment, and I didn't feel like driving all the way to her house and coming back to my apartment. I didn't want to miss the phone call from Mr. Chester. In the eighties, we had call forwarding and pagers. No cell phones. I needed to get home to my phone. I told my mother I would pick up my car the next day.

Later, in the wee hours of the night, my stepdad called. My eighteen-year-old brother had just had an accident in my car. *What?*

"What's he doing in my car?" I asked frantically. He avoided the question and told me he was coming to pick me up and take me to the accident scene where my car was. It was the first time I had ridden in the custom van. Seated in the back was my brother, and two of his friends. The tow truck driver was there when we arrived. My car was totaled!

It was December, a week before my Christmas break. My mother had given my brother my car keys without my knowledge or permission. He'd invited his friends to joy ride in my car and totaled it. Then, she hid behind her husband instead of facing me herself. She never acknowledged her wrong or apologized for it. After six months of enjoying my wheels, I was back to walking the back alleys to and from work. Me and a big stick, praying I didn't run into a big dog or a crazy person. And she, nor my stepdad, ever offered me a ride. By April, I had a new car, no thanks to my mother. Yet, she was back to taking it over, or demanding that I run her errands. Ugh!

In March of 2006, I asked my mother if we could move in with her once I sold my house. They had five bedrooms and was using just two. My son would not have to transfer once we moved into our new home because the children in my mother's development went to the same school as the children in my new development. This is crucial for children with developmental delays. Moving period, was traumatic for him.

I'd had a colleague of mine paint a life-sized mural of his favorite cartoon characters, Buzz Lightyear, and Woody on his bedroom wall when he was six. One day, I walked past his room and heard him talking. When I entered, he spoke in a sad tone.

"Mommy, they won't talk to me."

He thought they were real. How cute! At ten years of age, as we were packing to move, he lamented that he would miss them. I took his picture standing next to them, so he'd have them forever. Asking her this question in March was a step of faith. I hadn't even put my house up for sale yet. Hadn't even spoken with a real-estate agent. I ignored her forced, "Yes."

The previous two times we'd had the house on the market, we had no takers—not one. The first time it sat on the market for six months. The second time for a whole year. I hated the school my children attended, which is where I worked. We had to go, or I was going to catch a case! When I put my house on the market at the end of May, it sold in three weeks! I had multiple offers and sold it to the highest bidders. This, and the timing was the hand of God. I say so because as long as school was in session, we had somewhere to go all day while the steady stream of potential buyers traipsed through my house.

Accepting a bid the day before the last day of school meant that we weren't inconvenienced during summer break by having to vacate the premises, and find somewhere to go while the house was being shown. My real estate agent insisted that I remove all pictures of us, along with the black art on my walls. I know he definitely would not have wanted us to actually be home during a showing. I won't elaborate on the bias that such a request presents. I wanted to leave and whatever I needed to do, I was willing to do it. My real-estate agent was African American, and he knew the market and the game. I would suck my teeth every time he took me to a home that was for sale, and I'd see the family pictures prominently displayed. They didn't have to hide who they were.

I'd spent five years remodeling my house, inside and out. Amongst the many upgrades were new windows and doors, siding, roof, and new kitchen remodel (I still miss that kitchen by Four Season Sunrooms). There was an added sunroom with cathedral ceiling, remodeled bathroom that my stepdad did (he was very good with his hands. He'd owned his own upholstery shop). He replaced everything except the tub. Bath Fitters did the tub. I had new flooring, paint, floor to ceiling storage unit, toilet, sink and vanity. I even replaced the switch plate to match the new lavender and white color scheme. My detached garage even got a new facelift. Inside and out. As much as I loved all the newness, I was severely unhappy there.

My mother seemed so helpful. She'd accompanied me to the builder's office as I was purchasing a house that hadn't been built yet. She was there on moving day of my previous home, making sure they didn't waste time, as time is money. She showed up the next day to help me clean the empty rooms and prepare them for the new owners. She was so helpful, that when a colleague was selling tickets to *The Color Purple* on Broadway, I bought two. I treated her to dinner at a nice restaurant around the corner from the theater. It was a great evening. A month later, I made settlement on my former house and moved in with her. It was five months of hell.

My mother did a "Dr. Jekyll and Mr. Hyde." She yelled at me daily so badly, my eight-year-old daughter said, "Mommy, I don't like the way grand mom talks to you."

When I politely asked her to stop talking to me so disrespectfully, she dug her heels in and got worse. The very next day, as I ate breakfast, she plopped down in front of me with rules about cooking and cleaning. She later accused me of not buying groceries, eating her food and using her detergent. Even after I gave her my receipts to prove that I had bought the things she said I hadn't, she refused to look at them, and continued to falsely accuse me. She told *everybody* I was lazy, trifling, and God only knows what else.

Everybody was so nasty to me and my children. She hated me, and she wanted everyone else to hate me, too. If she could convince everyone that I was a horrible person, her hate would then be justified. People who used to speak or call me, stopped. Even my brother who lived there didn't speak. Acted just like his mother. Once she got in folk's ear, the relationship was over! Not once in those five months did she ever ask how the house was going. My stepdad did. And he even accompanied me when I had to go and choose where I wanted all the electrical outlets to be.

One day, I convinced her and everyone else to come see my unfinished house. The framing had just been completed, and the stairs installed. When we pulled up to the house, everyone got out and went inside, except for my mother. She remained in the van the whole time we were there. She refused to come inside.

I was so overwhelmed! Working every day, two kids, and a house that I had to pick out everything for. Flooring, appliances, cabinets, etc. I thought my mother would've shared this phenomenal experience with me. If I had a mother. This was a jealous demon, who could not find anything kind to say, or do, when it came to me and my children.

Wrath is cruel, and anger is outrageous; but who is able to stand before envy?
Proverbs 27:4 KJV

Four months in, my stepdad sat me down to talk. My mother was not home so he used the opportunity to encourage me.

"Tracy, I know it's not you; it's Vicky," he said. "She always acts like this this time of year."

"This time of year?" I asked. James' birthday wasn't until New Year's Eve, and it was mid-November. My mother was known to get *in a mood* around my deceased brother's birthday.

"She's been treating me with hate since I moved in in July!" I exclaimed.

I'd gone to my church's women's retreat a month prior. The topic was *subjection*. God was speaking to me. Every speaker spoke about being subject to the authority over us. From husband to supervisor, to laws, etc. and everything in between. They'd spoken of how painful subjection was, but how much more important our obedience to God's Word is than our own comfort. I'd committed myself to being respectful and subjective to this demon in my parents' home. I stayed away from her, and most of what she asked, I did. And my stepdad took notice.

"Well, just keep holding on." he said. He confided a whole lot of things about my mother that night. Her infidelities, and the reason for their first (of many) fist fights. I don't condone domestic violence, but what he told me was very disturbing. He'd walked in the room to find my mother repeatedly punching my sister in her face. "Y'all were so little then" he said. Between two or three years old. When he yelled at her to stop, she looked at him as if to say, this is *my* child, and punched her again. That's when my stepfather lost it and wailed on her. She was a mess, I thought, as this man who I was never allowed to get close to, lovingly supported and encouraged me. Things he'd never done in my mother's presence. My mother had changed my birth certificate and my sister's birth certificate to bear his last name, not even our real father's name. She told us to call him Dad. But this was the first time he and I had ever had a conversation like this. It was as if he was apologizing and purging himself of all the craziness between the two of them, all the years since they first got married at the tender ages of nineteen and twenty-one. He died eight months later.

My mother must have found out about our conversation or something, because the very next night, she punched me in the face, again. She was in my face yelling about something. She planned this fight. She was mad as ever, and I couldn't tell you what it was about. The devil never admits the real reasons for his sneak attacks. But I suspect her anger boiled over when I didn't run down to the jailhouse when she called to tell me how much my brother's bail was a week prior. Where was *her* money? After all, her husband was paying all the bills.

Not one of my brothers had lifted a finger to help me move, but I was always expected to give them whatever they wanted. My mother said once that the reason she had daughters first, was to help her with her sons. No dear, that is not why you had daughters first. This same brother who needed bail money still owed me a whole lot of money at the time. And it was a five-year-old debt. I was told that my mother told him he didn't have to pay me back. That saying about mothers who love their sons, but raise their daughters, could be tweaked in my mother's case. She *loved* her sons and *hated* her daughters.

My mother played favorites, and she didn't care about expressing it. I heard a preacher say that jealousy turns into hate if not dealt with. Hate turns into violence if not dealt with. I was forty-four, fighting my mother again. Nine years after the first time. My husband was not there to stop it this time. Every time I pinned her down, she got right back up like the Energizer bunny to charge me again. She couldn't beat me and was angry because she couldn't. I was so out of breath at one point, I sat down. When she got up off the floor, she snuck me from behind — a punch to my right jaw. I wasn't trying to hurt her. But she was trying to hurt me.

She clamped down on my thumb so hard, punching me repeatedly, as I tried to protect my face from her blows with my one loose hand. Finally, I chomped down on her breast, and she let me go. My thumb was purple from clotted blood for over a month. My stepdad couldn't stop us; he had emphysema and could barely breathe. He'd just yell, "Tracy stop, that's your mother!" Finally, he told me to take my kids, who'd been sitting at the kitchen table the whole time witnessing this horror, upstairs. I let her have the last hit.

"Get your shit and get out!" She yelled. I told her I was not going anywhere. When my stepdad wouldn't put me out, she told him he wasn't shit.

"You tell her!" She'd yelled to her husband.

"We told Tracy that she could stay here until her house was finished. We're not putting her out in the street this time of night with two young children," he responded.

The following Sunday, our pastor preached 1 Corinthians 13. All about love (charity). Later that day, my mother walked in the rain for three hours. It was pouring outside that day. I rode past her as she walked along the curb, hood to her coat over her head, and no umbrella. She looked silly. She was wrestling with that Word! That sermon had stepped all on her toes. I know it did. We hadn't spoken since our fight.

When she got back inside, she insisted we talk. I was so disappointed when she said, "If you ever put your hands on me again, I'm going to get a restraining order!"

"*What?* I did *you* a favor. If I had called the police that night, it would have been *you* that they dragged out of here in handcuffs—not me. You started the fight, not me!" My stepdad told me to turn the other cheek.

"Why should I act like Jesus while she acts like Satan?" I asked. "You are not gonna pummel me while I just stand still and let you. I am too old and have been through too much!"

Much more was said. At my stepdad's insistence, I apologized, I cried, and we hugged.

After I moved out, she'd hug me in front of everybody whenever she saw me. She'd never even held my hand the whole time I lived with her, let alone hug me. But to be honest, I longed for my mother's hugs. I didn't protest. When I lived with her, whenever I walked into a room she was in, she'd roll her eyes, and huff and puff; or look at me with such contempt. Can you imagine looking into your mother's eyes every day and seeing hate? It took counseling and much prayer before I finally walked away from what my counselor termed an abusive relationship.

"Why do you keep subjecting yourself to the abuse? This is going to drive you crazy. You need to be whole for your children." The Holy Spirit gave me 2 Timothy 3:5, after listing all my mother's characteristics, it says, "from such turn away." That was in 2008. It would be another five years before I was done for good.

"Emotional Abuse is an attitude of entitlement, and profound disrespect that discounts the inherent rights of the other person to dignity, separateness, and autonomy. It is characterized by great subtlety. It leaves no obvious marks that would call attention to injury, danger or the need for intervention. It's impact is insidious and pervasive. It strikes at perception, cognition, identity and the

very soul of the object of its persecution." From <u>The Abuse Beneath Abuse</u> by Barbara W. Shaffer in *Christian Counseling Today*.

We were going to a concert and my brother was going to watch my kids for me. When we got to my mother's house, the children jumped out of the car and ran inside ahead of me, as they always did. By the time I got in the house, my mother had already grabbed my sixteen-year-old son by the front of his shirt and dragged him upstairs into the back room with a belt. When I flung the door open, her back was to me, and he was facing me. Because he was sixteen and stronger than her, she couldn't beat him; so she condemned him to prison, and to hell. That was worse than a beating, I thought. I told my son, "Come on, let's go." Then she got up in my face.

"What are you going to do?" she said.

"You should have talked to me first. I'm going to pray!" I said. Wrong answer. She didn't believe in that. She had always taken matters into her own hands. This wasn't the first time she took a belt to my son.

When he was just six, she locked the bathroom door and beat my son so badly, he had black and purple bruises all over his body. I wasn't there when it happened. I noticed the bruises later when I was putting my children to bed. He refused to tell me who beat him like that. I must have asked him five hundred different ways. Days later, my stepdad told me what she'd done.

"She beat him pretty bad, Tracy." I could see that. My son's crime was that he was brain damaged, and as a result, had issues with hygiene. Six years old. I know some boys who *aren't* brain damaged and have hygiene issues. I confronted her and told her not to ever put her hands on my son again.

"He is developmentally delayed! He cannot do certain things as well as everyone else yet."

"Ain't nothing wrong with him!" she retorted. I could have had her arrested for what she'd done to my son. When I told her this, she screwed up her lips as if losing her job and her pension meant nothing to her. Days after the second belt incident, she was at my house with her Bible, trying to convince me that we needed to fast forty days and forty nights to dispel this demon that my son supposedly had. He'd watched some porno movies at her house a month prior when he'd spent the weekend. She'd gotten her cable bill and saw them on there. I told her that we could have paid her entire cable bill.

There was no crisis. No one had to be rushed to the hospital. Why did she always overreact to everything? Ruined our evening at The Dell Music Center to see The Stylistics over this nonsense. Over something boys his age do all of the time. Heck—boys, girls, men, and women! Don't get me wrong, I was quite upset with my son and punished him, but I was more upset with my mother. I reminded her that when she was my son's age, she was *having* sex, not just watching it like my son had done. After all, that is why I was here. She was sixteen when I was conceived, and turned seventeen, a month and a half before I was born. She then implied that my father raped her. A lie to avoid facing her own actions. I told her that that was a horrible thing to say about a man who was no longer alive to defend himself. If it were true, why hadn't she said anything way before now?

"I do not believe that," I said as I waved my hand. I told her she needs to beat on, and worry about her *own* sons, and their sexual promiscuity, as they, too, had most likely watched pornography as well.

"No, they don't!" she yelled. I ignored that and stated the name of her former lover who followed her to Camden from Denver, Colorado.

"I don't want to talk about that," she said, as she grabbed her Bible, and made her way out of my front door. It was 2013, and I didn't speak to her again until 2015, when my son, bless his heart, handed me the phone after he called her.

"Here, Mommy; talk to grand mom, and don't be bougie," my son said. We had spoken just twice from that time until we met in her dining room in June of 2017.

So, now here she was claiming to want her family back together again, while still harboring that devil inside of her. "No thank you." "I love you, but no thank you." Get rid of the demon first. She asked me about a book she gave me to read. She wanted it back. You know how like when children ask for their ball back because you won't play the game the way they want it played. We never did meet at my mother's for prayer.

He that loveth father or mother more than me is not worthy of me...

Matthew 10:37 KJV

On my son's birthday the following month, my mother and brother paid us a surprise visit. She apologized for how she'd acted at the funeral five months prior. I hugged her and told her that I loved her. And just like that, we were friends again. In December, when my mother asked if she could ride with me to pick up my daughter from her college dorm, I said yes. After nearly two hours into our trip, my mother stated that her mother's death was a suicide. *What?* This was disturbing news.

"What makes you say that?" I asked. She went into this crazy tirade about how my uncle's wife only ate hot dogs, and my uncle only ate salad. My grandmother was living with them at the time in Florida. She did not eat hot dogs or salad, so she refused to eat. Huh? Then my mother let out a chuckle that was most disturbing, as if she were saying—which in part, she did, that it served her mother right. I was so disturbed by this that I vowed to limit my time with my mother. Her conversations about our relatives were always so toxic. What confused me the most was that I'd never in all my life, ever heard my mother say one bad thing about her father. Not once. Ever.

Her father had separated from them, which my mother seemed to blame her mother for. He did not support them financially. His money went to liquor and all his loose women. My grandmother had put herself through nursing school so that she could take care of her children. She was a registered nurse in the ER for over thirty years upon her retirement. I still admire her for that. My grandparents never divorced, and my grandmother never dated. When he died in the 80's, they were still married. He was a drunk, who had fathered more children outside of his marriage to my grandmother, than he had within his marriage. I have an aunt who is just one year older than me, and she told me that her dad—my grandfather, was forty-five years old when he dated her seventeen-year-old mother. Oh my.

On the ride back to my daughter's university a month later, my mother was bragging about my brother's ten-year old stepdaughter. She was such a great basketball player. According to my mother, she was the best to ever dribble a ball.

"I go to all the games!" she exclaimed. "And Darrien is the best coach."

"Did you ever come to Chayil or Charis' basketball games?" I managed to ask when she finally took a breath. My daughter's team had gone all the way to the championships. She had played on the same court as the Philadelphia 76ers. My mother's response was an angry "No!" This no had five syllables. And her tone. She might as well have said. "*Hell no!* Why would I do that?" I turned the radio up, letting her know that I was done hearing about somebody else's child when you have never been as supportive and excited about the two blood-related grandchildren riding in this car with you.

In July of 2018, my children and I went to visit my mother. I was feeling nostalgic and wanted my children to see my childhood photos. We were looking at photos and talking when my mother began her combative rant about me not coming around the family.

"Why should I come around this family?" I asked. I reminded her of how mean *this family*, along with *her*, had been to me and to my children. I was the outcast, the black sheep of the family. The one everybody loved to hate. Family is not always the people that share your bloodline. Family should be people who *always* enjoy your company. Respectful. Have your back, loyal, supportive, etc. And *this family* was not any of that. Thanks to her.

"You didn't do anything to them. You just grew beyond the limit they set for you and that got them so mad. Forgetting that God (Elohim) sets the limit not man! Keep growing! Keep pushing and keep trusting God! Only God has the final say!"
~Women of Prayer, Instagram post, 5/16/2020

She brought up foster care again. Ugh! And brought up more of what Kacy told her about me and Mr. Chester — again. She totally missed the fact that I was standing right there, visiting with her. Looking at old pictures, revisiting old memories. Sharing the past with my children. She was so hellbent on starting an argument. She was not happy unless she was stirring the pot.

I would see my mother two more times before her unexpected death four months later, on November 29, 2018.

She was much more pleasant those last two times. Although it was not the relationship I'd longed for, I was appreciative that the Lord had allowed my heart to be open enough to accept what it was in the end.

"Love and devastation go hand in hand. Because it is impossible to get inside of a relationship and think that to find the depths of relating, that you can find the depths of relating without being challenged with pain. You have to have the clarity to understand who is worthy of us walking with them, and when it's time to walk away. Not everybody you love is meant to be the person you build a life with. Sometimes you have to love them from over there. You can love them, just from over there. But you can't love somebody else more than you love you. Ever."

~Jada Pinkett Smith, Instagram video post, 8/13/2018

Hurt people hurt people. Emotional abuse is far more damaging than physical abuse. Your physical wounds more often than not, heal. But the ramifications of emotional abuse are everlasting. My personality and character were shaped by my mother's bitter tone, her hateful sneers, eye rolling, and her huffing and puffing, whenever I entered the room. Not to mention the awful beatings. My sister said once that our mother would walk past her oftentimes and slap her upside the head for no reason.

My mother did not have the natural affection one has for their offspring. No hugs or kisses. "Get away from me!" or "Go outside (to play)," were her usual retorts when I came near her as a child. Her mockery and disrespect towards me in front of others, all made me feel that I was the worst person on the face of the earth.

I was in my forties or early fifties before I saw my value. I tolerated so many poor relationships and poor behaviors from people because I did not value myself. Abuse and mental health issues can be healed. Hallelujah! It takes commitment and obedience to undo the great harm that has been done. I still battle depression from time to time. Each year, however, it lessens. The generational abuse and curses must end! The good that has come out of my suffering is that I heaped all the love I had to give, but never received, onto my husband and children. I have told my daughter that she is pretty from the day I first laid eyes on her. It isn't hard to say because she is a very pretty young lady. Her eyes fixate on mine when she enters the room. I make sure that I am smiling. She is looking for approval. I don't want her to look for it in hell-bound men, like I did so long ago. Like so many young women are doing because they lacked the love they should have received growing up.

I have hugged and kissed on my children so much, that one night, my twenty-three-year-old son gave me a kiss when he came home from work. Happy to see his mom. I gave my children all the love I never got from my mother or father. They are two emotionally happy kids, and I have the Lord to thank for that. I asked Him long ago to help me love them and raise them so they would never feel about me, the way I felt about my mother.

Treat people the way that *you* want to be treated. Go to counseling. Preferably, a Christian counselor who will enlist the help of the scriptures and the blessed Holy Spirit, the Ruach Ha'Kodesh, and Elohim to guide your heart into peace and forgiveness.

> *If a man says, I love God, and hates his brother, he is a liar: for he that loves not his brother whom he has seen, how can he love God whom he has not seen?*
> 1 John 4:20 NIV

The word "brother" in this text could mean sister, parent, child, relative, stranger, acquaintance, coworker, boss, etc. Everybody!

By this shall all men know that ye are my disciples, if ye have love one to another.

John 13:35 KJV

Chapter Six

My Stuff

In the wee hours of the morning, I cleaned out my drawer next to my bed. I wondered why I had so much junk, and why I can't get rid of clutter. My stuff did not make the journey.

Almost ten years old when we moved from Denver back to Camden, New Jersey, my sister and I tore through the boxes, trying to find the box that held our toys, our treasures—our stuff.

"Mommy, where's our stuff?" We asked, almost hysterical. Our dolls, coloring books and Mrs. Collins' address were all in that box. Mrs. Collins was our fourth grade teacher. The only Black teacher we had had at Columbine Elementary School. She was moving to Boulder, Colorado, and gave the whole class her new address so we could stay in touch.

"I couldn't bring it," my mother responded unapologetically. My heart sank. My sister and I had learned through many beatings and cursing, not to show remorse or anger for the unbothered way in which our mother treated our concerns and belongings. We suffered in silence. Why didn't she tell us that she could not afford to bring our stuff? I could have put Mrs. Collins' address in my pocket and carried my dolls onto the bus with me.

To this day, we hold onto things way past their expiration date. Food, broken jewelry, trinkets, bills, toys, papers, junk mail, people, etc. Every summer, I go through the same boxes, bags, and drawers pouring over the same stuff, making some leeway in throwing some things out, only to make room for new stuff. Recycling things I never use, or look at again, until next year when I decide to go through this pile, and organize this stuff, again. And again, and again, and — what a waste of time! *If I could just let it go!*

Perhaps my over-consumption of things can also be attributed to my grandmother's seemingly unhappiness with anything that gave me joy. My sister and I lived with our grandmother from age ten to age twenty. She was an active member of her church, a registered nurse, an excellent seamstress, artist, and the best sweet potato pie baker in the world! She sold her pies, and people just could not get enough of them. I loved my g-mom, and she loved us, but she had some giving ways that irked me to no end.

She had seven siblings, and one of her brothers had a house fire. He, his wife, and their four children came to stay with us temporarily. I loved my cousins; but I also loved clothes. When my grandmother demanded that I give my cousins the few second-hand garments I had, I was sick. These girls have *both* parents. I'd only seen my biological father twice, and the most he'd done for me, was buy me a cheese steak hoagie, and treat me to a movie I was too young to appreciate or understand. My mother was on welfare with four kids. By the time my domineering grandmother had guilted me to death, questioning my Christianity and what not, my lackluster wardrobe was diminished. Was I being selfish?

Fast forward, I was a senior in high school still playing with Barbie. I loved Barbie! I was not even embarrassed when a male classmate of mine walked through my living room with a relative, as I was sprawled on the floor with Barbie and her camper, lost in the world of make-believe. Weeks later, my grandmother demanded that I surrender my Barbie and all her accessories to my younger cousins. *What?*

"I'm not allowed to play with Barbie?" I asked.

"You're too old for Barbie!" she retorted. "Give that *stuff* to your little cousins. You don't need to be playing with dolls!" I was an honor student, so Barbie was not interfering with my studies. Would she rather I had played with boys? Get pregnant like my mother did when she was a teen? Barbie was more than play for me; it was an escape! Escape from my unhappy, miserable reality. Next thing I remember is handing my prized possession over to two girls whose father was an engineer, and whose mother was an educator. They were the only blacks in their neighborhood, and the only black kids in their school. Their parents could certainly afford to buy them dolls. Why did they need mine?

But alas, the only item I have from my childhood in Denver that did make the trip (besides my memories) is a pair of scissors. Round-edge, silver scissors. Child-proof scissors. I could look at the irony of this in two ways.

1. Scissors Cut. Cuts are painful. Cut from a team, cut from the group, cut out of the picture, the cutting and molding that Jesus does with us during the transformation process — ouch! As a young child, I'd witnessed my mother stab her husband in the back with a pair of sharp scissors.

2. Scissors Create. My scissors never caused pain. I used them to cut out my paper dolls and their paper clothes. I used my scissors to make my paper dream houses. We glued notebook paper together to create the rooms. We cut furniture from the Sunday circulars and glued couches, kitchens, tables, etc. to the rooms as we saw fit. I could spend all day doing this. Imaginative play circa 1960s. A lost artform.

Scissors, like secrets, can be used for good and for bad. It depends on the person whose *hand* they are in. Can I get on my soapbox for a minute? It is a shame that computer games don't leave a lot of room for imaginative play. Our children are glued to a screen of some sort, for most of their day if we let them. Absorbed in whatever world they choose—fantasy or reality (social media). This has created a generation of social misfits.

Parents shove technology into tiny hands so they do not have to be bothered with their children. The gadget has become the babysitter. Recently, the discipline committee at my school, of which I am a member, convened to discuss the bad behavior of a third grader. He wasn't allowed to have recess for the following two weeks because he couldn't keep his hands to himself; however, his father didn't want to take away his video game. A video game that is notorious for its violent content. Parenting has really gone down the drain in the past ten or twenty years, as parents have been made to feel as if disciplining their children is criminal. The book of Proverbs is laden with wisdom about disciplining children. See also Deuteronomy 8:5 and Hebrews 12:6-7.

Chasten thy son while there is hope

and let not thy soul spare for his crying.

Proverbs 19:18 KJV

I still have most of my children's toys from their childhood. Maybe because I do not have anything left from my childhood? Shh! Don't say anything, but sometimes I catch my grown son playing with his toys still. Please do not tell him I told you. My daughter gave up dolls for tech gadgets long before she reached middle school. I kept all her dolls, along with my own collection. Barbie included! I love dolls! I am a doll collector. I have even participated in two doll shows! That was so much fun!

I have most of my children's school papers since preschool. I needed them for the scrapbooks that I was supposed to give them when they graduated from high school. But I have not finished them yet. Still got all my grade books from thirty plus years of teaching, along with other memorabilia from my career in education. My stuff also includes textbooks from college and graduate school, along with some of my college papers and presentations.

Thinking about downsizing makes me sad. My stuff defines me and tells my story. How could I ever get rid of my stuff? My *Essence* Magazine collection, paintings, not to mention my clothes, shoes, bags and jewelry! I'm also keeping the clothes that do not fit for when I finally lose weight! (sigh) Well, I don't have to downsize yet, just thinking about it.

My Stuff

10/15/2018

My stuff is as vast as the sea, important because
it belongs to me. My stuff defines a life lived
well, an interesting story it has to tell. My stuff
isn't old, isn't used, isn't new, don't worry
about it, it's for me, it ain't for you.
My stuff includes knickknacks my children broke during play,
kept them, shoulda glued them, shoulda throwed them all
away. But I liked them too much to have to part, they hold a
special, sentimental place in my heart. If this is wrong then
God will help me see, that my stuff, my things, are just a
miniscule, minute, milligram, of who the Lord, is making me.

Chapter Seven
Friendship

*A friend loves at all times…*Proverbs 17:17 NIV

Most people do not know what being a true friend is. They sling this word around carelessly to describe people who cater to all of their whims, whether right or wrong. Or to fool people they actually hate. People even use this word to describe non-committal sexual relationships they are in. "Friends with benefits." Whenever I want to know the definition of something, I always go to the Bible. God's Word is the standard by which we live, and do, and be. (Acts 17:28)

There are just two words that define friendship. But powerful words they are.

1. Love – *verb showing action. To have affection for.* 1 Corinthians 13:4-8 KJV defines love: *Charity suffereth long, and is kind; charity envieth not; charity vaunteth not itself, is not puffed up, Doth not behave itself unseemly, seeketh not her own, is not easily provoked, thinketh no evil; rejoiceth not in iniquity, but rejoiceth in the truth; beareth all things, believeth all things, hopeth*

all things, endureth all things. Charity never faileth: but whether there be prophecies, they shall fail; whether there be tongues, they shall cease; whether there be knowledge, it shall vanish away.

If your "friends" and even relatives, don't display these characteristics, then throw them away, because they are not your friends, and they will do you harm—sooner or later. Just look at the train wrecks on these reality shows. Are those misguided groups of *Housewives* really friends? Proverbs 10:12 says, "... love covereth all sins." If your girlfriend (and/or relative) is running her mouth and exposing all your business to Lottie, Dottie, and errrybody, honeyboo, she ain't yo' friend. Love doesn't expose your wrongdoings. Love keeps them hidden.

He that covers a transgression seeks love; but he that repeats a matter separates very friends.
Proverbs 17:9 NIV

Love cares about your feelings. (See Proverbs 4:1-9 for more information.) I'd shared something very personal with an older woman who I thought was a friend. A few personal things that I had not shared with anyone else. Just her. And one day, my mom told me to stop telling this woman my business because she was a gossip. And to prove it, my mom repeated what I had told to this woman only. Wow. Was I disappointed.

2. All – means all. Not sometimes. Not many times. Not most times. All the time! All the time being kind. All the time covering you, etc.

Pastor Paul Sheppard[2] helped me understand friendship better when he said, he does not need fair weather friends. Because our life isn't always fair weather. There are storms, hurricanes, and tsunamis in this life. If you can't weather the storm with me, don't expect to chill with me when the sky is blue and the sun is shining.

There are people who will only show up when you are doing good. But soon as you experience any trials, tragedies, or trauma, they disappear, only to reappear when they think the coast is clear. If they are your friend today, they should still be your friend twenty years from now. And if they were your friend twenty years ago, they should still be your friend today.

They went out from us, but they were not of us; for if they had been of us, they would no doubt have continued with us: but they went out, that they might be made manifest that they were not all of us.

1 John 2:19 KJV

My friend Debbie and I met in college. She was a very pretty girl born in Trinidad. Her family had moved to North Jersey when she was younger. I begged my grandmother if she could be her boarder as she needed a place to stay, close to school. Rutgers didn't have dorms at the time. We were close. We'd lost touch for many years after college.

When my husband was dying in the hospital, she called. She'd still had my grandmother's phone number, and my gmom had given her my number. Boy, was I happy to hear from her! And what timing! We caught up. She was married with a young son. I promised to visit her once my husband was home and doing better. By the time she called again, my husband had just died, and I burst into tears over the phone. She was so sorry to hear the tragic news. She sent my children a couple of outfits. Wasn't that nice? But I lament that I wasn't emotionally able to keep in contact with her. Our friendship was a true friendship. I prayed for us to reconnect one day and stay in touch forever the next time. Guess what? She found me on Facebook in February 2020! Thank you, Lord, for answering my prayer. I have my friend back!

Love never fails, and since friendship is defined by love, friendship never fails. Folks scattered when my husband died. Scattered like roaches when you turn the lights on. My tragedy enlightened me about who my ride or dies were, and who they were not.

When people show you who they are, believe them.

- Maya Angelou

In high school, I considered Karla my "BFF." We giggled our way through ninth grade algebra. And when the senior prom rolled around, it was Karla who came through for me. My prom date asked me to the prom the day of the prom. Yup. I hadn't planned on going. But during physics class, Todd asked me, and I said yes. Karla just happened to have a few gowns and offered to loan me one for the occasion. My grandmother made me a white all-lace shawl as she thought the spaghetti straps on my powder blue gown were too revealing. Rounding out my ensemble were my eggshell-colored Easter shoes. My mother did my hair and makeup, and off I went. Todd picked me up two hours after the prom started. Something about having to wash the rented car. I didn't have a perm, so by the time we got to the prom, the Jersey humidity had nearly swollen my hot-combed locks into an afro. Todd had on a white ruffled tuxedo. We had to have been the most mis-matched couple in the history of high school proms. But that didn't stop us from spending most of the night waiting in line to get our picture taken.

Todd's mother worked at our school. They lived in the suburbs. He had a driver's license and a car. He and I started dating right after graduation. Every time I got in his car, Karla and two other friends joined us. We had big fun! First time I got drunk was with these four friends. Todd wanted us to see who could guzzle the most cans of Olde English 800. I was drunk before I finished the first can. Todd beat everybody by drinking most of the two six packs he bought, and he was the only one of us with a driver's license.

When Karla and I slid down the wall onto the floor at the party we went to that night, Todd quickly helped us up off the floor, out the door and into the car. He drove us all safely home. He was good at holding his liquor. Todd had an inground pool at his house, so Karla, my sister, and I often went to his house to swim. Karla would often tease Todd, which I didn't like, but I never mentioned this to her. On one such occasion, she and the other two friends had ribbed him so much, he got mad and drove to McDonald's. He got out of the car, went inside, ordered food, sat and ate it while we waited for him to return. We didn't have any money for McDonald's.

"Tracy I don't know what you see in him! Look at him. Look what he's doing. He didn't even buy you any food." said Karla. As time went on, Todd wanted more than a platonic relationship, and I wasn't interested in that, so we broke up. I heard through the grapevine that my friend Karla and her cousin were regulars at his house, swimming in his pool. I wondered what else she was doing with him besides swimming in his pool.

Years later, Karla and I ended up working together. Despite going behind my back with Todd, I naively thought that we would still hang out together. When she didn't hang out with me, I questioned her, and she made it seem like she was doing her clique a favor by choosing to be with them. The ish hit the fan when a mutual friend and coworker of ours stopped speaking to me.

"What did I do?" I asked. She reluctantly told me that Karla had told her, that I had slept with her guy. What? When I asked Karla why she'd told her that, she said the guy had said it. Well since dude worked with us, I angrily marched right up to him and told him to stop lying on me, and to keep my name out of his mouth. Things were cleared up between my friend and I, and neither of us could believe what Karla had done. She had viciously tried to destroy our relationship.

Wow. A true friend would never go to another person with a hurtful tale about you that they have no proof about. And even if it were true, a *true* friend wouldn't throw you under the bus like that.

A *friend* of mine was having her first child. We'd known each other since I was ten. In our twenties at the time, she'd made me her daughter's godmother. She all but admitted I was her choice because I had a job. She spent most of *her* life collecting welfare. My sister and I owned the house we shared, and we were both teachers. I guess I seemed like the best person for the role. I knew that being a godparent meant that I was responsible for teaching the child about God, ergo, the term *godparent*. But my self-absorbed friend, who was an only child and spoiled by her mother, was under the delusion that I had accepted to step in financially, while the father of this baby had stepped out.

She expected me to foot the bill for all of her daughter's milestones. I was expected to help her plan her daughter's first birthday party. I even hosted a party for her at my house once. When my goddaughter was three years old, I'd asked if she could go to church with me. The answer was always no. For the sake of not sounding like a pervert, I stopped asking.

My friend never encouraged a relationship between her daughter and me. Whenever I came around, she was always at a friend's house. This didn't stop her mother from calling me out of the blue with, "Freda needs..." or "such and such costs." From the venue to the item, I was expected to meet the financial need. I wrote a letter of recommendation for my goddaughter to attend the best high school in the city. She got in, and when it came time for her senior prom, I got the call to let me know that she "needed" a gown. I ignored the financial implications. I'd asked my friend to remind me of the date and time of her prom so that I could see her in her gown. The call never came.

"Oh, I forgot" was the excuse, as I looked at the prom pictures with all her other friends, who obviously hadn't escaped her memory, sharing in the pre-prom send-off. I gave my goddaughter a large sum of cash on her high school graduation day, after her mother lamented that she "needed" this exact amount for her class pictures. After all, you have to have graduation pictures. And Freda was such a pretty girl. I've never received a graduation picture, so I guess the money was put to some other use.

One day as I shopped for school clothes for my children, Freda's mother ran around the department store looking at clothes. It was an unexpected stop on our way to the movies. I thought she was looking for clothes for her youngest daughter, until I approached the cashier. She ran up to me with a whole outfit for herself.

"Tracy, can you get these for me? I'll pay you back."

It's been over a decade, and she has never even tried to repay me for the outfit she wore to her high school reunion. Two years after Freda graduated, my friend called me out of the blue, at Freda's request, to tell me that Freda was six months pregnant. *Oh dear, here it comes,* I thought. For the next several weeks, I would get a series of calls about the venues she was looking into for the baby shower. I knew she was waiting for me to jump in and say that I would pay for it, but that never happened. Freda gave birth before her mother decided on a venue for the baby shower...at a bar. A ratchet dive that was eventually shut down after someone was murdered there.

Anyhoo, when my friend called to inform me that Freda needed a stroller, I knew this was the end. Why couldn't I show up to the shower with twenty dollars in a card? Why was I expected to buy the most expensive gift for a person I *hardly* knew? After all, I was a widow with two children, a hefty mortgage, and a host of bills. I never went to the shower.

I haven't heard from either of them since. When someone comes at you with "I need..." Run! Don't walk! Run for your life. Because they are *takers*. They don't care about you. They only care about what you can give to them.

Ronda and I met through our sons. She was several years younger than me. Our boys were in the handicapped preschool disabled class together. She walked up to me and said that we should exchange numbers so that our boys could have play dates together. When I went to her home, I witnessed to her about Jesus while our children played. I invited her to attend worship services at my church. She came, and she and her two sons joined!

Her husband, who was genuinely nice, did not come to church. Ronda spent a lot of our phone conversations complaining about her husband. She was a stay-at-home mother, yet complained about the lack of money they had, and other habits of her husband's. They lived two blocks away from me, and I'd enlisted the help of her husband a time or two, to take my children to school along with his son, when I had to leave early for a work-related workshop. They eventually moved to another town. Ronda's attitude changed. The friendly, young lady I'd known became distant.

She became uppity, like I was beneath her now that they were living elsewhere. Her son had spent the night at my house, they'd come to multiple birthday parties, and barbeques at my house. Ronda ate up my homemade sautéed crabs as if she'd bought them herself. But now, she barely spoke to me when I'd see her and her boys in church. I found out that she had not told the new school that her son was classified. She was completely *brand new*. Until a few years later when she saw where *I'd* moved.

"Can I borrow $500?" was her response in the foyer of my newly built home. She was serious. And I loaned it to her. My motive was completely wrong. I wanted her to see that she wasn't better than me, that in fact, she was nowhere near better than me. Especially after I saw where she was living. It only backfired, and for the next several years she begged for money. I must add that through tears, she apologized to me for the way she had acted. I appreciated her apology, especially since I wasn't used to people apologizing to me for their offenses. However, even after I told her she needed to get a job when her youngest son started school, she continued to beg. There was no reason why she shouldn't work.

"After all," I told her, "You have a husband and I do not."

We prayed for the Lord to bless her with a good job and He did! With benefits! A great job! A couple of times when she worked holidays, I babysat and fed her two hefty-sized boys, who were teenagers at the time, and over six feet tall. When she got off from work, I had a plate for her, too. I gave her furniture, two couches, and a dinette set and clothes that were never worn. Having a job did not deter her from continuing to beg me for money, even after I told her that I was not loaning her any more money.

She called me at work crying, saying that she needed nine hundred plus dollars for an electric bill. Sorry, can't help you there, hun. She called again, asking that I co-sign for a $1,300 loan. Nope. Nada. When she wasn't begging for money, she was crying snot and tears about her life and her husband. All I could do was listen and pray for her. In all those years, she never reciprocated any of the kindness I had extended to her. My son had never spent the night at her house. We'd never been invited to a party or barbeque. Oh, there was that one time she called me to invite us to her youngest son's birthday party, *after* it had already started. I could hear all her *invited* guests in the background over the phone. After I told her how inconsiderate she was, I hung up. She thought it was funny. And she certainly never gave *me* a thing, not even a thank you card. A taker in the truest sense of the word. As long as I had something to give, she was right there to take.

It'd been a few years since we'd seen each other on this one particular sunny Palm Sunday morning. She'd told me a few years prior, that she'd gotten in some trouble at work, and she'd also suffered some injuries. She eventually was fired. In the past few years, I had been neck deep in my own turmoil and torment, and hadn't the time or energy for *her* drama.

As we walked into church together, having ran into each other in the parking lot, she asked about my daughter, who was a freshman in college at the time.

"Oh, she's doing fine. She made the Dean's List last semester!" I responded.

"Well, at least you have one that's intelligent." *What the what now?* Before I could respond, two familiar faces jumped into view and greeted me. After my hellos, I looked around and Ronda was gone. I wanted to give her the benefit of the doubt. Maybe she was lamenting about her own sons. Both had struggled academically. We met because her son was in the same class with my son, which meant he had some intellectual issues, too. And that $1,300 loan she wanted me to co-sign for, was for a learning center for her youngest son.

I wanted clarity, so I called her the next evening. She didn't answer. I left a pleasant, brief message to call me back. About an hour later, she returned my call.

"Hello?" I greeted.

"Did I do something wrong?" she angrily asked. She was geared up for a fight, I could sense in her tone.

"Well, you tell me. What did you mean when you said—" Before I could finish my statement, she flew into a rage and screamed into the phone.

"I didn't say that! I would never say that! Somebody else said it!"

"Why are you screaming at me?" I asked.

"Because you are calling me up, accusing me of something I didn't say. Tracy, that is a horrible thing to say." I hadn't even completed my sentence, so what was she referring to? Guilty conscience. "Our boys have known each other for a long time..." she went on. Blah, blah, blah, I thought.

"You did say it and you know you did. Why would you say something like that about my son?"

"I didn't say it, *you* said it!" And with that, I cursed her out. All of Camden came out of me. I out screamed her and hung up. She had lost her mind. All that I had done for her no good unappreciative, narcissistic #*%@! Wow. Is it really that hard to admit you are wrong and apologize?

On Thursday morning, she called me while I was at work.

"I'm gonna do the forgiveness thing," she said. The night before at Bible study, pastor taught on the subject of forgiveness. That we ought to forgive those who trespass against us. The Lord was speaking right to me. Only I wasn't ready to forgive just yet.

"I apologize for yelling at you on the phone the other night," she went on. Apparently, my slow friend did not understand "the forgiveness thing."

"So, let me see if I have this right. You are apologizing for yelling, but not for what you said?"

"Tracy, I didn't say that. I would never say that." Her tone was much softer.

"You know there was a time when I thought you were my friend. We have known each other since our sons were three years old, and now they are twenty. I would never make a disparaging remark about your children. I do not accept your apology. I yelled at you, too, and I am not sorry. Since you have a hard time admitting what you've said and apologizing, don't call me anymore." And with that, I hung up, blocked her number, and removed her from my contact list. In the years since, I have forgiven her. But we will never be friends. She crossed a line you just don't cross.

A fellow church member approached me to let me know that she did hair. She was the same age as I, and our birthdays were just a few days apart. My daughter and I became her clients. When I asked her to do my daughter's hair for a wedding she was in as the flower girl, she gave me a seven a.m. appointment on the morning of the wedding.

"Can you do my hair too?" I asked. The bride, my coworker, had asked me to be her assistant during her wedding, so I was going to be seen by everybody. I wanted to look my best.

"No" was church lady's reply. No explanation, just flat out, *no*. You mean to tell me that at seven in the morning, she couldn't do us both? But I didn't press her. My loyalty as *her friend* hindered me from canceling my daughter's appointment and finding a place where we both could get an appointment. Needless to say, I never got my hair done professionally for the wedding.

A few years later, she emailed me asking for a ride to an evening church meeting. We were in the same ministry, and I had given her two rides before to meetings.

"I'll find you when it's over," she said the last time I had given her a ride as she sauntered clear across the other side of the room, as if sitting next to the person who provided her with a round trip, door to door service, free of charge, was beneath her. It had been nearly two years since I'd seen or heard from her, despite the fact that we lived within walking distance of each other. This time I was annoyed. I deleted the e-mail and never responded. After all, she had proven to be a very *unfriendly* person.

A few years prior, after I'd spent several hours in her scorching backyard, socializing at her daughter's high school graduation party, I started the climb up her deck stairs. I was looking for a reprieve from the hot sun, and maybe a cup of cold water.

"Oh no, I already have people in my house." *What?* I can't come in? Was she mad because she no longer was my hairdresser? Or was she really treating me like I was totally insignificant to her? I've had many barbeques at all three houses I've mortgaged, and I have never told any of my guests that they couldn't come into my home. Most people clamor in the kitchen anyway. Jersey summers are *hot* and *humid*!

After descending her stairs, I got into my car and went home vowing to never darken her doorstep again. Sometime later after this graduation party debacle, she called insisting that I help her with a ministry-related task. The task involved me lifting a very heavy bag. Her husband had done the lifting for her, yet I was expected to do my own lifting. I tried to appeal to her sense of compassion. I am a woman and after all, she knew I was widowed with two small children, with no one to help me do the heavy lifting. But she didn't care. When I refused, she angrily threatened to complain to our ministry leader. At the next ministry meeting, the leader, who was also a client of hers, sneered directly at me the whole time she lectured us about fulfilling our obligations in the ministry.

This is some bull (in Bernie Mac's voice), I thought. I never went to another ministry meeting while she was the leader. And so, here I was reading this request she sent in an e-mail after tattling on me along with all the other unfriendly things she'd done. I'd given her rides to church even after she'd refused to do my hair for a wedding. She tried to walk past me without speaking the Saturday after I'd deleted her e-mail, but I called out her name.

"Hi, church lady."
"Oh, hi Tracy! Did you make it to church on Wednesday?"
"Yes, I did", I said.

"Well, it worked out. Julia called me that afternoon to get her hair done because she was going out of town. So, I didn't make it because I did her hair."

Did you catch that? She missed prayer meeting to do her *real* friend's hair the *same day* she was asked. But she wouldn't do mine for the wedding, even when I'd asked several days in advance. A real friend, one who *loves* at *all* times would've cared about how I looked for a wedding. And a real friend wouldn't have done all that other slimy stuff either that this one had done.

I met "Miss New York City Slicker" one summer while volunteering at Vacation Bible School. We shared teaching duties in the same class with three other women. She came off as very needy. She was a single mom with two children living at home. They were younger than my two children. She had two adult daughters and a grandson who lived in other states.

She and I were the same age. She was a teacher like me and commuted from her home in South Jersey to Harlem, New York each day where she worked. We even drove the same exact cars. Different colors, but the same make and model. We seemed to have a lot in common. She seemed aloof most times while voicing her need for rides for her children to different places throughout the week. I took her son to mentoring meetings along with my son, picking him up at his house and driving back to the town where I lived for those meetings. She would pick him up from my house after the meeting, on her way home from the Greyhound Bus station.

She talked a lot about her ex-husband in a way in which always made her out to be a victim. She didn't believe in disciplining her children, so whenever her son or daughter had a disagreement with her, they would call their dad in New York to complain. He would get on the phone and fuss at her about the issue. I told her that she should stop entertaining those ridiculous phone conversations where he'd always treat her as if all of her decisions were the worst to make. She had the kids most of the time, and he only saw them every other weekend.

"Your house, your rules," I'd said. But I also noticed after months of listening to her recount the dynamics of her marital relationship, that her behavior as a wife may have left her ex-husband feeling a bit betrayed and disrespected. Anyhoo, *she* was my friend, not him.

The following summer after we'd met, she'd insisted that we go to the church picnic. I hadn't gone in many years and wasn't excited about going this time. However, she was persistent.

"We can take the children and have a nice time!" she exclaimed. So, the Sunday before the Saturday picnic, I handed her the money for me and my children, and she bought our tickets. By Wednesday, I hadn't heard from her, so I gave her a call. We needed to get our menu together of the food we'd planned to take, among other things. The school year had ended for me, but she was still working. She told me that she just found out that she had to work the weekend and would be staying in New York through the weekend.

"Can you take my children to the picnic with you?" She asked. I was livid! She knew all along that she was working that weekend, and she expected me to babysit her children for her. Without even coming right out and asking. She played me well. Teachers don't find out that we're working outside of our contractual hours three days beforehand. Programs and activities that take place outside of school hours must be school board approved, and the board only meets once a month. Teachers working those programs must be approved by the school board as well.

I hung up, and when she called me repeatedly on Saturday, I didn't answer. I wasn't going to the picnic if she wasn't going, and I certainly wasn't taking her ill-mannered children, who I really didn't know very well. She left several messages, all of which went ignored. To this day, she insists that she didn't know she was working when she took my money. I didn't believe her, but we managed to get past it, without her ever paying me back.

When she invited me to a Fourth of July party at a friend's house in Harlem, I felt she was trying to make amends. So, I agreed to go. After church, she picked me up and we headed down the road. She told me that she'd also been invited to her friend's boyfriend's house in South Jersey. So maybe we could go to both.

"Why are we stopping here?" I asked as she pulled into a Boston Market restaurant.

"I'm hungry," she said.

"We're gonna eat at your friend's house, right?" I asked. She ignored my question as she ordered a complete meal. I thought, well it *is* a two-hour drive. So, I ordered a sandwich. I didn't want to spoil my appetite at her friend's house in New York. She finished all her food and announced that she needed to get her hair done. She suggested that I get my hair done, too. So, we headed all the way over to northeast Pennsylvania to a Dominican shop where they burn your hair bone straight. She was so into the conversation she was having on the phone that she hadn't noticed that the non-

English speaking young lady who'd completed her hair had made her pin curls too small. Miss New York City Slicker, who I'll call "Miss NYCS" for short, made her take them all out and make them bigger.

It was a little after 5 p.m. when we finally left the salon. *We can still make it to the party in New York, but we must get going*, I thought. Just as she slid into the driver's seat, she announced that she had to go to the Cherry Hill Mall in New Jersey to get some concealer.

"What? When are we going to New York?" I don't remember her answer, but at the mall she insisted I get out of the car and go into the mall with her.

"You're only buying concealer. That shouldn't take long," I reasoned.

"Come on, Tracy," she responded. I decided to go to the shoe department, my favorite department in Macy's, while she headed to the makeup counter. *What is taking her so long*, I thought after a while, but I was enjoying myself too much to find out. One pair of purchased shoes later, I went looking for her. Oh my God! She was sitting in a chair getting a full facial beat.

"What are you doing?" I angrily asked. "You didn't say you were getting your face made up." She ignored me as she directed her makeup artist to find the right shade of red. The shade on her lips just wouldn't do. I was so angry, I called my sister to complain. I knew we weren't going to New York. She had settled on the backyard barbeque at her married friend's boyfriend's house. If I'd known that, I would've changed my white blouse that I'd worn to church earlier that day or stayed home. When she finally finished, she doused herself with the sample bottle of her favorite perfume, and out the door we went. I am so longsuffering. And naïve.

At the dude's house I chatted all evening into the night with her friend's sister and nephew. They were a delightful pair. The food was pitiful. I so missed my stepfather's cooking. He was a master chef and griller. He'd created his own barbeque sauce once and had bottled it. Don't know what ever happened with it. My Texas-born stepfather was good at a lot of things. They don't make them like him anymore.

A week later, Miss NYCS slipped and said that she was supposed to meet some guy at that Fourth of July barbeque, but he never showed. She dragged me around all day so she could meet some dude? That explained her excursions to the salon and the mall. When she called a few days later, I let her have it. Told her about her deceitful, conniving ways. She wanted to come over to talk. She cried and apologized. She told me that her ex calls her a liar in front of her children. I was appreciative of her apology; I wasn't used to getting apologies.

Most people who offend you, get offended when you confront them about their offenses. Shame. My mother and sister had done some pretty slimy things to me, and my mother rarely ever apologized. My sister has never apologized for any of the treacherous things she's done to me, but believed I deserved her ill-treatment. So, when Miss NYCS said she was sorry, I believed her, and resumed our friendship.

The following summer, Miss NYCS called me one day and told me that her daughter had driven her car to work without her permission. She wanted me to drive her van, and she would get her car and drive it back home. Her daughter would have to find another means to get home. By the time we got back to her house, her seventeen-year-old daughter was already there.

"No! I'm not giving you back your keys. You left me to find my own way home!" her daughter yelled back at her when my friend asked for the keys to her car. My friend reminded her rebellious teen that she had offered her a ride earlier that day, and she had turned her mother's offer down. As my friend was at the barber shop with her son, her daughter seized the opportunity to steal the car.

They went back and forth for what seemed like twenty to thirty minutes with my friend begging for her keys and her daughter telling her no. I couldn't take it anymore. By the time I got to the top of the stairs, this girl was on the phone with her dad, expecting him to take her side. He was on speaker, so I heard him tell his daughter that what she did was wrong, something about not being insured, that her mother's car could have been seized if the girl had been stopped by police.

"Give your mother her keys!" he yelled. This man wasn't so bad after all I thought. She was still holding the phone when I pushed the red button to disconnect the conversation.

"You heard your father. Give your mother her keys so I can go home! Enough is enough!"

"Who are you?" She asked as she disappeared into her room. She knew *very well* who I was. She'd eaten at my house on Thanksgiving and came to my daughter's graduation party. I'd been to her house multiple times. I decided to head down the steps before my temper got the best of me, and I found myself explaining to a judge why I killed this insolent girl. Just as I got to the bottom of the stairs, my friend's son came down with the keys. Behind him, my friend's daughter yelled from the top of the steps to me.

"Who the fuck are you?"

"Who the fuck are you?" I responded.

"You fat bitch!"

"You retarded bitch!" I countered.

"I hope you die of diabetes!" she yelled, as I walked out of the front door. I thought it best to exit before I ran up those stairs and give her the whooping her mother should have given her years ago. My friend remained silent throughout this disturbing exchange. I had been a teacher for over thirty years, and I can't recall any student I ever taught who'd spoken to me with such disrespect. Perhaps I shouldn't have responded the way I did, but I guess you had to have been there. To witness a child speaking to their mother with such hate and insolence. I was not raised that way. My friend was shook by her daughter's behavior and insisted we drive her car to a friend's house so this demon-possessed child couldn't do damage to her car while she took me home.

She had a photo album of her deceased sister, and other keepsakes in her car that her daughter had destroyed out of meanness. I've already quoted several Scriptures about disciplining children. *Reread please.* This is what happens when you don't discipline your children when it is called for. In the following year, my friend sent her ill-mannered daughter to Paris, the prom, and gave her a graduation party; however, she never insisted that she apologize for what she'd said to me.

Miss NYCS's birthday was a few months later. She'd invited a few friends to go with her to her favorite dinner and jazz restaurant in Atlantic City. All six of us piled into her van. The only other male besides my son, did the driving with his girlfriend in the passenger seat. We pulled up to the gas station and Miss NYCS insisted that one of *us* pay for gas. No one thought this was right. But I paid anyway. We got to the restaurant and everyone was responsible for their own meal. I paid for two — mine and my son's. I'd also bought her a card and a gift. Whew! I am a nice friend, aren't I?

Well, eight months later, my birthday rolls around. Two days before my birthday, Miss NYCS asked me what my plans were. I told her I wanted us to go to Warmdaddy's in Philly, which is another jazz restaurant. She voiced her resentment and reminded me that her favorite spot was in Atlantic City. *Not your birthday, ma'am.*

The day before my birthday, she called me to ask if I wanted to go to a birthday party the next day. She'd just gotten an invitation to attend her adulterous girlfriend's husband's birthday party on the same day as my birthday. This is the same friend we'd visited on the Fourth of July instead of going to New York. Now, this friend was back with her husband. No longer with the boyfriend because he wouldn't—now get this—*commit*. Hahaha! What in the world? I reminded her of my plans and asked her why would I go celebrate a stranger's birthday on *my own birthday*? I texted her later that evening to let her know the exact time of my reservation at Warmdaddy's. She responded that she had a prior commitment and for me to have a nice time. Wow. The next time I saw her in church, I refused to speak to her.

"I know you're not that selfish," she retorted. *What the what!*

"Narcissists think it's disrespectful when you don't let them disrespect you."

~@narcissist.sociopath.awareness2

For I say, through the grace given unto me, to every man that is among you, not to think of himself more highly than he ought to think; but to think soberly, according as God hath dealt to every man the measure of faith.

Romans 12:3 KJV

I am so happy I went to Warmdaddy's with my children! Patty Jackson, a radio host, handed me two free tickets to see Jill Scott and Boyz II Men at the Mann Music Center on the lawn. They have drawings every Friday night, and I was one of the winners! What a terrific birthday present! Having lawn tickets was significant because I was able to buy another lawn ticket, and my children and I were able to sit together. We had an amazing time in all that heat! And it was packed!

We eventually got past this latest debacle, and resumed this dysfunctional friendship, only for me to endure her sly insults and take her daily calls all about herself. When I rebuked her for walking out of the salon and stiffing the stylist—*my* stylist, the one I'd referred her to, she blew up. She told me it was none of my business, that she was grown and could do what she wanted. The reason I knew about it was because she'd called me multiple times from the salon to complain that he was taking too long. After he'd installed a full weave into her head, she decided she wasn't going to pay, and called me again from her car in the parking lot. I told her to pay and complain to the manager, but she didn't. She played the victim. Wrong as two left feet.

> *Faithful are the wounds of a friend; but the kisses of an enemy are deceitful.*
> Proverbs 27:6 KJV

That was the straw that broke the camel's back. I was done. If we cannot pull each other's coat about our wrongs, then this really isn't a friendship. Tell me my slip is hanging, or that my zipper is down, cause then I'll know that you care about me. Others will laugh and talk about seeing your slip below your skirt, and your belly (or worse) through your opened zipper. They are not friends. Friends have your back! We aren't right all the time, and our friends should keep us in check when it is needed. Now, if someone is always pointing out negative things about you, and never appreciating you, then they are not your friend. Proceed with caution or give them less of your time.

My pastor said that his friends cannot be friends of his enemies. How true! Have you ever told a *friend* about someone you didn't like 'cause they had treated you badly, then watched as your *friend* and this other person became close? What kind of foolishness is that? Give them the benediction. They are not your friend.

Church folks can be some of the messiest people I know. Satan shows up at the church first 'cause that's where God's people are. Correct me if I'm wrong, you Bible scholars out there, but just about every time an evil king, or a heathen nation took Israel captive, they always set up altars to Ba'al. Satan's influence is in the churches, in the pulpit, the choir, the officers and members. Church is not a building! The church is the *people*. The *ecclesia* (Greek) means, "called out; unity." The body of Yahushua Ha'Mashiach (Jesus Christ). We ought to be as the church of Philadelphia, Revelation 3:7-13.

I know thy works: behold, I have set before thee an open door, and no man can shut it: for thou hast a little strength, and hast kept my word, and hast not denied my name… Because thou hast kept the word of my patience, I also will keep thee from the hour of temptation, which shall come upon all the world, to try them that dwell upon the earth.

Revelation 3:8, 10 KJV

Wherever there are people, there are bound to be problems. People and problems go hand in hand. You can't escape problematic folk. Unfortunately, I could go on and on about the folks I mistook for friends. I've grown quite a bit, so these takers and fakers don't get very far with me anymore. You live and learn.

"You don't lose friends. Most of the time, you lose people who never liked you in the first place. God is making room for the right ones." www.REALTALKKIM.com

"Never re-friend a person who tried to destroy your character. Forgive them and love them in the balcony."

@RealTalkKim

I made this mistake with Karla who I mentioned before. About twenty-five years after she stabbed me in the back with her lie, we began hanging out together through a mutual friend. We had been friends on social media for a decade by 2020 when she plopped into the comment section of my post. Karla proceeded to tell me that I was ruining the politician's reputation in a video that millions of viewers agreed was disturbing. She claimed to not see what we all saw and told me through a back-and-forth debate, where she was trying to justify and explain his actions as innocent, that I was wrong.

Ha! The nerve. I blocked her and told her friend who joined her in the comment section, that she'd had a heck of a nerve telling me of all people that I was ruining the reputation of a man who couldn't care less what we posted, who didn't even know, or cared that we existed. She tried to ruin *my* reputation so long ago, someone she did know and pretended to be friends with. The audacity! Obviously, her hatred of me was still a fire in her heart that she had never reckoned with.

I harbor no ill will against these women. I have forgiven and moved on. Tupac once said, "Just because you lost me as a friend doesn't mean you gained me as an enemy. I am bigger than that. I still wanna see you eat, just not at my table." If you see yourself in any of the people I've written about here, *stop*. Repent. Ask the people you have hurt or offended for forgiveness and start exhibiting the characteristics of a true friend. Proverbs 18:24 states, "A man that has friends must shew himself friendly: and there is a friend that sticks closer than a brother." A (true) friend loves at all times (Proverbs 17:17). A good friend is like a good bra; they lift you up, and never leave you hanging.

Chapter Eight

Why Do The Righteous Suffer?

But the God of all grace, who hath called us unto his eternal glory by Christ Jesus, after that ye have suffered a while, make you perfect, stablish, strengthen, settle you.

1 Peter 5:10 KJV

I started writing this book in August 2018. Around that time, the three pastors I listen to all preached a sermon on 1 Peter 5:10. It was confirmation that I was doing the right thing in writing this book, with this title and this theme. So many people struggle with the concept that Christians suffer. I've heard preachers say that Christians are in one of three places during any moment of our life:

1. Headed toward trouble

2. In trouble

3. Coming out of trouble

Oftentimes, our struggles are far worse the closer we are to Yahuah, than when we were while running around deep in sin. When we commit fully to Christ, it is imperative that we put on the full armor of God, because our enemy (Satan) seeks to destroy our witness for Christ. He doesn't want others to be converted by accepting Jesus Christ as Lord and Savior (John 3:16).

Ephesians 6:11-17 KJV says, *Put on the whole armour of God, that ye may be able to stand against the wiles of the devil. For we wrestle not against flesh and blood, but against principalities, against powers, against the rulers of the darkness of this world, against spiritual wickedness in high places. Wherefore take unto you the whole armour of God, that ye may be able to withstand in the evil day, and having done all, to stand. Stand therefore, having your loins girt about with truth, and having on the breastplate of righteousness; and your feet shod with the preparation of the gospel of peace; above all, taking the shield of faith, wherewith ye shall be able to quench all the fiery darts of the wicked. And take the helmet of salvation, and the sword of the Spirit, which is the word of God:*

We who serve the Lord are the Bible that the world reads. Our words and actions are under scrutiny by those outside of the church, and even *in* the church. Someone once told me that, "We have been picked out to be picked on."

Yea, and all that will live godly in Christ Jesus shall suffer

persecution.

2 Timothy 3:12 KJV

This verse doesn't say that we *might suffer,* or that we *could suffer.* It says that we *shall suffer.* It is a given. It is our birthright as born-again believers.

In John 15:18-21 KJV, Jesus said, *If the world hates you, ye know that it hated me before it hated you. If ye were of the world, the world would love his own: but because ye are not of the world, but I have chosen you out of the world, therefore the world hateth you. Remember the word that I said unto you, The servant is not greater than his lord. If they have persecuted me, they will also persecute you; if they have kept my saying, they will keep yours also. But all these things will they do unto you for my name's sake, because they know not him that sent me.*

The Lord sent a pharaoh to my school as the new principal about fourteen years ago. He is more than ten years my junior, and upon meeting me for the first time, he insulted me. He thought his role was to police me. I was and am a teacher leader as a math coach. This has come with much resentment, as I am African American and everyone else is white.

During his second year as principal, a colleague falsely accused a ten-year-old black student of being "high on marijuana." I complained to him in his additional role as the affirmative action (AA) officer (of all people). I simply asked him to tell this woman what the proper protocol was for suspected drug abuse, which didn't include spreading this lie throughout the entire school. She had slandered me just the year before.

I'd taught a group of students in her class an algorithm in computing fractions. They became master of it! They excitedly shared it with her, and she became outraged. Huh? She'd never seen the algorithm before and accused me of not teaching the content. To her, my bachelor's degree in applied mathematics and my secondary math certificate meant nothing. Not to mention, my master's degree in education administration along with an additional five certifications. More than any other educator in the district. Her prejudice wouldn't allow her to admit that my math knowledge trumped hers. She, like all the other elementary teachers in the building held only elementary education degrees and certificates. She threatened those six fifth graders with failure if they didn't compute the fractions the way *she* had taught them. When I requested a meeting with the union about her ignorant, slanderous statements, they sided with her. Yup. Birds of a feather *stick* together.

Anyhow, I knew the student well, and knew he was not guilty of her accusation. My mother sold marijuana when I was younger. I know what it smells like, and I know what being high on it looks like. He didn't have the smell or the look. Very nice young man from a Christian family. Needless to say, the principal did nothing. He was young, arrogant, and seemed to lack any knowledge of the responsibilities his job demanded. He found out that I would teach the math lesson in this teacher's absence, which was something I did out of kindness, not out of duty or obligation. He came in while I was teaching and told me it was my formal observation. He accused me of ignoring the raised hand of a white student I had mentioned in my AA complaint. Wrote this false accusation on my formal observation document, along with the child's name.

Of course, I attached my rebuttal accusing him of being vindictive because of my AA complaint, which is against the law to retaliate against someone who complains about a coworker. To his credit, he did the right thing and removed that lie from my observation form because he didn't want the superintendent to read my rebuttal. Weeks later, when I entered the building, he was waiting for me. Five teachers came to him demanding that he do something about the fifth grade drug addict. In racists' minds, all black people are drug addicts or drug dealers, despite that the largest group of opioid users and overdoses on opioids are white people[3].

He had met with this teacher and her union rep. Told her what I'd asked him to tell her weeks ago, without the formalities. He knew her accusations were false he said because "Tracy told me..." Threw me right under the bus. Why mention me now? Or at all? He told me and her that if he were to have this student tested for drugs and the test came back negative, he and the school board could be sued. I was so sorry I had told him anything and vowed never to do it again.

He allowed any and everyone to sit in his office and complain about me. He infringed on my due process rights by calling me into his office to tell me what they said so he could lecture me about affective communication. Please. The nerve. A couple years later, I finally told him that this is not a plantation and that I was not a slave. With that, I stormed out of his office and over to the superintendent's office. Didn't get any satisfaction with him. The principal wrote me up. I had never been disciplined in all of my twenty-four years of teaching at that time.

This was the fourth school I had taught in, and he was the third principal we'd had at this school. My crime? I told a group of teachers that I would not create the form they asked me to create.

"No," I simply said. "What do you do for me?"

It may not have been the right thing for me to respond with, but that is how I felt at the time about women who always found fault with me, and who had a friend in him. The curriculum director came to me a week later and told me there would be another meeting because they didn't think I understood the gravity of what I'd done. They were trying to break me. How dare I speak up for myself out of sheer annoyance of their bullying and disrespect!

I enlisted the help of my union at the county level. We had a second meeting, which infringed upon my rights. No new infractions had occurred. I'd already been disciplined with the write-up and threatened by the superintendent that my position would be in jeopardy if this second meeting didn't go the way they deemed fit. I was advised to remain silent as my union rep spoke on my behalf. I was furious! There was a second discipline write-up. The old boy network was rearing their ugly heads. But let me tell you about my Jesus! By June, the superintendent signed his initials to a form I created signifying that both write-ups were removed from my personnel file. We sat in his office as I looked through my file to make sure.

While our relationship is now in a much better place, he has spent most of his tenure here collaborating with everyone else when it comes to math—classroom teachers, the math coach at the elementary school across town, and the reading coaches, before he engages me about any of my ideas. If we had not gone into quarantine, there would have been a Math Night at our school that one of the reading specialists organized without any input from me.

For eleven years, our math program was a success, exceeding the state benchmark at times. God's favor was with us. The principal was so thrilled, he called my home during the summer of 2011 to tell me how proud he was of my hard work and dedication.

And whatsoever ye do, do it heartily, as to the Lord,
and not unto men;
Colossians 3:23 KJV

That September, they hired a new curriculum director who trashed everything I was doing in a private meeting with my principal. Our scores dropped that year with her mindless meddling. The following year, our math scores skyrocketed to 87% passing as a school! This time, he ignored me and gave all the credit to our textbook series.

If God be for me, He is more than the world against me.
Romans 8:31 (paraphrased)

I've been traumatized by the things I have endured in this life. Abuse, molestation, rejection, false accusations, unprovoked hate, being lied on, etc. I was tormented, and sometimes still tormented by the people I've loved the most. But when I think on God's Word, I can't help but smile.

Beloved, think it not strange concerning the fiery trial which is to try you, as though some strange thing happened unto you: But rejoice, inasmuch as ye are partakers of Christ's sufferings; that, when his glory shall be revealed, ye may be glad also with exceeding joy. If ye be reproached for the name of Christ, happy are ye; for the spirit of glory and of God resteth upon you: on their part he is evil spoken of, but on your part, he is glorified. But let none of you suffer as a murderer, or as a thief, or as an evildoer, or as a busybody in other men's matters. Yet if any man suffer as a Christian, let him not be ashamed; but let him glorify God on this behalf.

1 Peter 4:12-17 KJV

Verse thirteen says that we are partakers of Christ's sufferings, which means because He suffered, I suffer. And *if we suffer (endure), we shall also reign with him: if we deny him, he also will deny us:*(2 Timothy 2:12 KJV) Many people suffer unspeakable things. That does not mean they are suffering because they are Christ's.

...for He maketh His sun to rise on the evil and on the good, and sendeth rain on the just and on the unjust.
Matthew 5:45 KJV

Blessed are they which are persecuted for righteousness' sake: for theirs is the kingdom of heaven. Blessed are ye, when men shall revile you, and persecute you, and shall say all manner of evil against you falsely, for my sake. Rejoice, and be exceeding glad: for great is your reward in heaven: for so persecuted they the prophets which were before you.

Matthew 5:10-12 KJV

Be Blessed 9/6/2006

This will be a great year

Less sorrow and much cheer

Determined to live in peace and joy

Not gonna allow others to annoy

My destiny's certain and this is true
Trust in the LORD and He will guide you Yes, life is what happens while you're making other plans
But if you're a Saint your life's in His hands

It may not feel good or even great
Some things I have to deal with I loathe and hate
But be of good cheer and know this is sure you will be victorious if you just endure All the hardships this life is sure to dish out
So, start your day with a praise and a shout

Praise the LORD for what He allows

Praise the LORD for His awesome powers
Praise the LORD for His mercy and grace
the answer to prayers He gave in haste

Praise the LORD for the roof over your head The
protection as you slept when you rise out of bed
There is so much to praise Him for
Don't let man's sinful ways keep you from
opening the door of your heart to allow
Yahushua to sup with you
He hears our prayers and

He understands what we go through
He has an ultimate plan we know very little about

Be honored He uses us, don't sit and pout

SHOUT! SHOUT! SHOUT! SHOUT!

'til they ask if you're okay

then look 'em straight in the eye and say,
"Did you accept Yahushua today?"
"Did you ask Him to come into your heart?"

This is the great commission, this is our part
Do His will, He'll take care of the rest then
walk in His blessings all His best.

I have knocked on the doors of strangers in strange neighborhoods, passing out tracts. My children and I knocked on all our neighbors' doors handing out tracts. Those who were kind enough engaged us in conversation about salvation; others disappeared into their homes and refused to answer their door when they saw us coming. I've passed out tracts to strangers while traveling, while waiting in the doctor's office, and at the grocery store. Left them in hotel rooms with the cleaning lady's tip as I checked out. I passed out tracts to my colleagues. Invited many of my coworkers and friends to my church to worship.

Many came and went, and only a few stayed. I witnessed to the man who became my husband. I have taught Sunday school, and Vacation Bible School at three different churches. I've taught Bible study classes to middle schoolers and high schoolers. I've taught adults at my church on how to teach. I've been a faithful tither at multiple churches where I've been a member. I recently completed a year-long training course to become a lay counselor at my church.

> *But be ye doers of the word, and not hearers only,*
>
> *deceiving your own selves.*
>
> James 1:22 KJV (See also verses 23 and 25)

With all the people I have impacted for Christ, do you think Satan's minions wouldn't torment me enough to get me to shut up and stop doing ministry? The more you do for

Christ, the more you will be persecuted. And don't think like I did years ago, that if I stop working in ministry, the devil will leave me alone. Things got so heated in my life that I ended all involvement in ministry. I had no desire to do anything other than show up on Sunday morning, listen to the sermon, and go home. But the persecution didn't end. Instead, the Lord taught me how to *endure* it as a "good soldier."

"God gives His biggest battles to His strongest soldiers"

~Facebook post

Then I said, I will not make mention of him, nor speak any more in his name. But his word was in mine heart as a burning fire shut up in my bones, and I was weary with forbearing, and I could not stay.

Jeremiah 20:9 KJV

I don't profess to be the godliest person on earth; instead, I identify with Paul when he said, I am chief sinner (1 Timothy 1:15). We sin daily in thought, word, deed, motive, attitude and in action, as my pastor always says. Repentance is key! Turning away from sin and asking God to help us see our sins as He sees them. It is a blessing to be a "called out" one!

We are troubled on every side, yet not distressed; we are perplexed, but not in despair; persecuted, but not forsaken; cast down, but not destroyed.

2 Corinthians 4:8-9 KJV

There is hope! How do we deal with persecution without committing murder? Without going mad? Here are my thoughts:

Point #1

Be still, and know that I am God: I will be exalted amongst the heathen, I will be exalted in the earth.

Psalm 46:10 KJV

Be still. How many of you know that this is a very hard thing to do when someone is in your face, lying on you? Screaming at you, treating you with the utmost disrespect. Two of the worst principals I've worked with were so disrespectful to me at times and I'd argue with them. I didn't care who they were, they weren't going to treat me any kind of way. I'm not a brown-noser or a butt kisser. They wanted a control that overstepped their bounds, and I wasn't gonna give in to it.

Be still and know that I am God. Don't raise up. If they cheat you out of money, let them. If they pass you for a promotion, let them. If they lie on you, let them. I'm gonna borrow an old phrase and add a twist. When they (your enemies) go low, JESUS is high (and lifted up). No one is higher than He is, except the Father. Get quiet and prayerful. That confounds the enemy.

When the school administrators did not provide the same professional development, trainings, committee membership, and resources that the math coach at the other elementary school was always privy to, I went to the Bible. In Joshua 6:1-27, Joshua fought the battle of Jericho. Well, I marched for seven days around my school. Praying and praising the Lord for what He was going to do. I trusted the Lord to destroy the walls of secrecy and poor communication as it pertained to me. Each day at lunch time, I'd plug my earphones in my ears so the children and adults on the playground would think I was singing along to my iPod. Little did they know. I had to shoo away the occasional student who wanted to walk with me. God is so faithful to us when we exercise mustard seed faith. That was ten years ago as I write this, and there isn't anything that goes down that I don't ultimately find out about. God thwarted the plans of my enemies who tried to remove me from my position, by withholding pertinent information and resources from me. Let me tell you that the Lord has given me so much wisdom, that these folks come to *me* for information. And while they are hard pressed to broadcast my amazing accomplishments, I don't have a problem humbly bringing them up when it is fitting to do so. Speaking of being humble, being still requires humility.

- Humble yourselves in the sight of the Lord, and he shall lift you up. (James 4:10 KJV)
- And thou shalt remember all the way which the LORD thy God led thee these forty years in the wilderness, to humble thee, and to prove thee, to know what was in thine heart, whether thou wouldest keep his commandments, or no. (Deuteronomy 8:2 KJV)
- If my people, which are called by my name, shall humble themselves, and pray, and seek my face, and turn from their wicked ways; then will I hear from heaven, and will forgive their sin, and will heal their land (2 Chronicles 7:14 KJV).
- Likewise, ye younger, submit yourselves unto the elder. Yea, all of you be subject one to another, and be clothed

with humility: for God resisteth the proud, and giveth grace to the humble. (1 Peter 5:5 KJV)

- Humble yourselves therefore under the mighty hand of God, that he may exalt you in due time: (1 Peter 5:6 KJV)

Do you get it now? When we remain humble, and let the Lord fight our battles, He lifts us up in time. At the right time. When we raise up against our enemies, we are taking the fight out of God's hands. He's not fighting with you; He fights *for* you! And He does *not* need your help! Get back and let Him do what only He can do. You'll just mess things up for yourself. Every time!

Dearly beloved, avenge not yourselves, but rather give place unto wrath: for it is written, Vengeance is mine; I will repay, saith the Lord.
Romans 12:19 KJV

Point #2

Bless those who persecute you: bless and do not curse them.
Romans 12:14

A month before the world went into lockdown, a coworker of mine lost her natural mind. Her classroom was the meeting room, and I had emailed her to let her know that I would facilitate all day meetings with staff in her room on March 9th.

"You need to be out of my room by 3:00," was her response, among other things. I felt that her tone was a bit disrespectful. She used her room to entertain students at dismissal while they waited for their bus to take them home. I didn't respond to her email; but the next morning when I saw her in the hallway, I walked up to her and stated that my meeting might go past 3:00. Before I could say anything else, she immediately became enraged.

"Well, you need to get up and find another room to go in."

"No, I'm not going to do that," I said.

"Well, you need to talk to Ben! You need to talk to Ben!" She sounded almost hysterical. Ben was our principal. *Her friend.*

"No, I don't need to talk to Ben," I said, as I kept walking.

"You get back here, Tracy!"

"No!" I yelled back at her standing in the hallway.

"That's not fair. You can't walk away; I'm talking to you!" *Did she take complete leave of her senses?* I thought. Did she think I was going to engage her in a shouting match first thing in the morning? I was looking for a student who was supposed to be doing the morning announcements, and I didn't have the time or patience to deal with this woman and her nasty attitude.

Bless those who persecute you. I'd learned this years ago as the Lord was teaching me how to navigate in such a hostile working environment. He'd moved hateful people out of my path either through retirement, termination, transfer, and even death. This walk I have with the Most High is personal. He loves me, and cares about me. He does His best work in, and through us when we are obedient to Him!

Later that day, I emailed her to let her know that I made some changes and apologized for the confusion. She emailed me back and expressed her appreciation but wanted to talk. I responded that there was nothing to talk about. In my response, I also included how I had been very accommodating with her request a few weeks prior, when she asked me to babysit the bus students after school for her for three days, but her attitude was not reciprocal. And this, I stated, I did so despite how I felt about her. Next thing I know, I'm getting an email from a union rep in our building about a PR&R (Professional Rights & Responsibilities) meeting with the three of us. The union? Really? No, was my answer.

After going back and forth, a friend convinced me that I should meet, and tell this woman how despicable she is. She spoke first. Playing the victim and painting me as the monster.

When she saw my reaction to her lies, she got more confident, and angry in her storytelling. When it was my turn to speak, I reminded her that in the nineteen years that we'd known each other, she'd always had a nasty tone when speaking to me, as if I were a dog or something. I told her that her email was not nice. She tried to make excuses. I told her that her excuses were unacceptable, and that I had been very respectable of her. I've always given her what she asked, no matter what. I stated what had happened exactly the way it happened and stated that I am scheduled for meetings in her room only once. "How hard could it be to accommodate me past 3:00, when I did you a favor by watching bus students for you for three days? I said, *okay*, when you asked. Okay. I did not place any conditions on your request or answer disrespectfully. I simply said, okay."

She wanted to know what it was that I didn't like about her. I reminded her about how she would stare at my friend Vanessa during bus duty when there was eight of us in the multipurpose room during bus duty. Vanessa, a black woman from Camden like me, is a lunch aid and teacher aid. The children *love* her! As soon as they entered the room after school, they'd run up to her with hugs and stories about their day. This teacher *hated* this! Why do racist people hate to see a group of black people laughing and talking to one another?

She would glare at Vanessa, walk up to the students she was talking to, and without saying one word to Vanessa, would tell the children to go sit down. She ignored all the other children in the room to focus on the handful of children who were getting love from Vanessa. I was pissed about this and told Vanessa to speak up. Vanessa was not a coward. Quite the contrary. But like me, she's a Christian and wanted the Spirit to lead her actions. But some people make it extremely hard. After months of this disrespect by this hate filled woman, Vanessa spoke up.

"Why do you keep coming over here worrying about what I'm doing?" Vanessa towered over this woman who shrunk back, unable to answer her questions with the anger she'd been holding in for months.

"Yes!" I said to her, "Good for you!"

Shortly after that, I was in an assembly and another white coworker walked up to the group of black boys I was talking and laughing with.

"Move back!" She yelled at them. I never saw her coming. When I turned, she was practically out the door. I told the boys to move back up to me and we resumed our conversation. I couldn't get to this woman's room fast enough when the assembly was over. "Why would you tell a group of students that I am talking to, to move away from me?"

"Did I do that?" she asked. You sure did. To her credit, she apologized. I went straight to our union president with mine and Vanessa's experiences, and he promised to send a letter to the staff after he agreed that this type of behavior is unprofessional and disrespectful. When the letter came out, the bus duty coworker ran to her friend—the principal, to complain. Ben stood in the multipurpose room for three days, blatantly staring at Vanessa. He then summoned her to his office to tell her that he understood why the other woman had complained.

The following year, Vanessa and I were assigned bus duty in the library with four other staff members, monitoring the kindergartners. The disgruntled coworker stayed in the multipurpose room with five other teachers and the students in grades one through five. This was the first time ever, that students were separated in two different locations at the end of the day.

I threw all of that in her face during that meeting as she tried to justify her actions. A few times, we got into a shouting match and the union person had to repeatedly tell us to stop and calm down. I was heated! I was raised by a mean woman who loved to fight. But as S. Epatha Merkerson said in the 2005 film, *Lackawanna Blues*, "I'm a lady and I choose to act like one." I told her that I didn't want to hear her justifications for her poor actions, and that I'd never seen her walk up to another white woman and treat her the way she had treated Vanessa. She retreated. Defeated.

"Well, we're going to have to agree to disagree," she stated. Wow. Was she expecting me to act like I had wronged *her*? After the union rep said that I was *hostile*, and the other woman was *upset*, I was done. I questioned her choice of words to describe me, versus this woman with her arms crossed, giving me the evil eye. The union rep, also white, fixed her wording, then requested that I make a couple of changes. Only speak to this woman via email. No more talking by the by in person. And find another room for my last meeting. The angry coworker wasn't given any changes to make. I made a mental note not to do anything different. And I didn't. If I need to say something to her I will, whenever, and wherever, and all my meetings were held in her room. Period. Since our meeting, she is so pleasant to me. Shame it took all of that to get her to that point.

The lessons here are many, but I want you to see that I was able to be kind to her despite her years of hate. My ability to say yes to such an unlikeable person was not my flesh, it was the Spirit. She mistook my kindness for weakness. I had been very longsuffering with her and had exhibited other fruits of the Spirit with this woman and others on my job. I regret not telling her that my quick response to do what she asked came from my obedience to God's word, and nothing else.

> *But the fruit of the Spirit is love, joy, peace, longsuffering, gentleness, goodness, faith, meekness, temperance: against such there is no law. If we live in the Spirit, let us also walk in the Spirit.*
>
> Galatians 5:22, 23, 25 KJV

Ye have heard that it hath been said, An eye for an eye, and a tooth for a tooth: but I say unto you, That ye resist not evil: but whosoever shall smite thee on thy right cheek, turn to him the other also. Ye have heard that it hath been said, Thou shalt love thy neighbor, and hate thine enemy. But I say unto you, Love your enemies, bless them that curse you, do good to them that hate you, and pray for them which despitefully use you, and persecute you; that ye may be the children of your Father which is in heaven: for he maketh his sun to rise on the evil and on the good, and sendeth rain on the just and on the unjust. For if ye love them which love you, what reward have ye? do not even the publicans the same? And if ye salute your brethren only, what do ye more than others? do not even the publicans so? Be ye therefore perfect, even as your Father which is in heaven is perfect.

Matthew 5:38-39, 43-48 KJV

Point #3 - Forgive!

For if ye forgive men their trespasses, your heavenly Father will also forgive you: but if ye forgive not men their trespasses, neither will your Father forgive your trespasses.

Matthew 6:14, 15 KJV

You don't have to tell unremorseful people you have forgiven them. Forgiveness is a matter of the heart, not the tongue. I told someone that I forgave her for a terrible wrong she'd done, and she got angry with me and acted like she hadn't a clue what I was talking about. She was offended! How dare I throw her hateful behavior back in her face! It has taken me from a few minutes to years to forgive people fully of their offense(s) against me. It can be difficult, but we are commanded to do it (Matthew 6:14, 15; 18:21-35). Pray and ask Yahuah to help you forgive.

The weight that is lifted from carrying anger and bitterness toward someone is the best gift you could give yourself. Unresolved unforgiveness can wreak havoc on your immune system and health. I read once that a cancer patient went into her oncologist's office and the first question he asked was, "Who are you angry with?" Before he would start treatment on her, she had to deal with her heart issue. In an interview,

Dr. Charles Streeter stated, "The white blood cells – killer cells, are emotionally labile. If you have a bitter spirit, a hateful spirit, a stress, an emotionally stressful traumatic experience shuts those cells down for a period of time and they get a build up of cancer cells, and they go to a weakened area and create a tumor. In women, the cancer cells are found in the breasts, the uterus, and the ovaries. In men it's the prostate, and the rectum. These are irritated areas. In smokers, it's the lungs."

Chapter Summary

...after that ye have suffered a while, make you perfect, stablish (confirm), strengthen, settle you.

1 Peter 5:10 KJV

The purpose of suffering is to *strengthen* us. Emotional, spiritual, and psychological strength is gained from our suffering. God's Word is so much plainer to me when I'm going through trials and tribulations.

- When we see God's hand in our deliverance, time after time, we become *settled*. No more worries, anxiety, fear, and fretting when chaos is all around us. We personify the peace which passes all understanding (Philippians 4:7). We gain a confidence in God's ability to deliver us out of *all* our afflictions.

- When we can be still, bless our enemies and not curse them, love our enemies, do good to them, pray for them, turn the other cheek, speak to them, and give them what they ask or need, we have been made *perfect.*

Another reason for suffering, and the most important of all, I think, can be summed up in a statement that Job made at the end of his suffering.

I have heard of thee by the hearing of the ear:

but now mine eye seeth thee.

Job 42:5 KJV

My knowledge of the Most High is greater now more than ever. I understand His word better. I trust Him more!

Yea doubtless, and I count all things but loss for the excellency of the knowledge of Christ Jesus my Lord: for whom I have suffered the loss of all things, and do count them but dung, that I may win

Christ, and be found in him, not having mine own righteousness, which is of the law, but that which is through the faith of Christ, the righteousness which is of God by faith: that I may know him, and the power of his resurrection, and the fellowship of his sufferings, being made conformable unto his death; if by any means I might attain unto the resurrection of the dead.

Philippians 3:8-11 KJV

My prayer is that all we who suffer for the name of Christ, will be perfected in our suffering. Count it all joy!

Chapter Nine

Somebody Cared

With so much emphasis on the suffering that I have endured, I feel it is important to also write about some triumphs I have experienced. Here they are:

So many children in the foster care system have suffered some type of abuse. But according to my grandmother, our foster parents were genuinely nice people, who took great care of us. They even wanted to adopt us. Somebody cared.

I must use this opportunity to thank the welfare system. If you've never been poor and hungry, you cannot appreciate what a blessing this is. When my stepdad left us in early 1972, we had nothing. My mother could not afford to take care of four children by herself. One night, I laid awake crying and praying. I was so hungry. We hadn't eaten a meal in a while. Hunger is a feeling no one should ever have to suffer. Although, I know that many do. That night, I promised God through my tears, that I would be a *good girl* if He gave us some food to eat. The next morning, when I went to the kitchen, my mother was bringing in bags of groceries with people I'd never seen before. "Mommy, mommy, I prayed that God would give us some food, and He did!" I was so happy. Shortly after that, we all hopped on a bus headed for Philadelphia, Pennsylvania, leaving Denver, Colorado for good. My Uncle Alzie picked us up and took us home to Camden, New Jersey. My mother signed up for welfare and got food stamps. Food stamps saved my life! We'd go to the Italian market in south Philly once a month and get all kinds of food! Those excursions were the best. We had so much food, my grandmother would come over with her foil and plastic baggies and divide the food up to be given to other relatives. "Now Vicky, don't be like that," she would say when my mother would protest. My mother had a right to protest. She had five mouths to feed, and some of those relatives had not been kind to my mother, probably because of her waywardness. But my grandmother came from the days when black people shared what they had in order to survive. We never lacked, though. And we never went hungry again. I didn't keep my promise to the Lord, unfortunately. Haven't always been a *good girl*. But He kept His. Even my children have never gone hungry. 'Scuse me while I praise Him! Somebody cared! Hallelujah!

My grandmother did a lot for me, my mother, and siblings. She made many of mine and my sister's matching dresses, and outfits throughout our childhood. She'd made mine and my sister's eighth-grade prom gowns and graduation dresses. My first career choice was to be a seamstress. My two great aunts were seamstresses. They could sew very well. My aunt made me a suit one time. It was sharp! My g-mom bought my sister and I a huge piano and paid for lessons. She taught us how to crochet; however, I don't remember how to anymore. She wasn't the affectionate type, but she was proud of her twin granddaughters, and would always have us sing or recite poetry when her church groups came over. She was our Sunday school teacher, so we were in all the plays and activities. I shudder to think how things would have turned out without her. She was a "Florence Nightingale." Whenever someone got sick, they came right to my grandmother's to be taken care of. She nursed her younger brother who came to live with her when he was ill. She nursed her estranged, ornery husband back to health when he came to stay with her in the eighties. Very giving. She was a no-nonsense godly woman. Somebody prayed for me, and it was her! Somebody cared!

When I was in first grade I struggled with math. Two plus two is four was a concept I just could not understand. Or maybe it was subtraction. I don't recall. But I do remember my teacher, Ms. Sneaker. She was patient and gentle with me. Every day, I would cry during math, unable to understand those basic concepts. Despite the many children in her class, she knelt beside my desk and softly walked me through those problems. As a math teacher, I regretfully have not always been as patient, but I am grateful for Ms. Sneaker. I was seen by her. She made me feel like I mattered. Somebody cared!

When we were eight years old, my sister and I spent the summer in Camden, New Jersey with our grandmother. One day, our summer camp went to a lake for a picnic. My grandmother came with us with a basket of food, and a blanket for the ground. She told me not to go out too far. My sister and I had learned to swim the year before. I thought to myself, *I know how to swim; don't worry about me!* Being the hardheaded person that I could be at times, I went further out than anybody else. Now in 1970, there were no ropes that dictated the area everyone was confined to. I went to stand up and suddenly lost my footing, as the ground ceased to exist. I was caught in a whirlpool, spinning uncontrollably to my death, eyes wide open, mouth wide open and screaming. My nine-year-old cousin somehow managed to grab the back of my bathing suit, and slung me backwards, out of harm's way, without herself becoming victim to that whirlpool. Oh my, did I feel horrible! I must have laid on that blanket for the rest of the day. "Didn't I tell you not to go out too far?" I heard my grandmother say. Sometime in the wee hours of the morning, I woke her up. "Grandma, I don't feel so good." She called a friend to come and take us to the hospital where she worked. I spent six weeks in that hospital, sick as a dog! I had swallowed a lot of dirty lake water. They thought I had tuberculosis at one point and put me in the basement in quarantine for a short period. Those heavy metal doors to the rooms, with one little square window made it seem like I was in prison. It was scary down there. I couldn't have visitors down there. My grandmother visited me daily when I was in the pediatrics wing, during her shift as an RN. But she was not allowed to visit me while I was quarantined. I eventually regained my health. My Aunt Catherine took my sister and I back home to Denver, on the plane. My first airplane ride! The stewardesses made such a fuss over us. They gave us United Airlines wings to pin to our tops, coloring books, and crayons. My cousin saved my life! Somebody cared!

I was seven or eight years old. It was summer, and we were walking through the alley to get to the street. We were headed to the playground. My sister and friends were ahead of me, already crossing the street. I thought I would run the rest of the way, not stopping to look both ways before I crossed the street. Just before my foot hit the curb on the other side of the street, I heard, a loud, screech! "Come here!" There were two elegantly dressed, black men sitting in a fine convertible car that had barely missed hitting me. They were probably in their late twenties or thirties. Looked like they had gone to church. Fine looking gentlemen. Only, the driver had an angry, mixed with concern, look on his face. I looked both ways before I ventured over to this car parked in the middle of the street. The driver put his arm around me, and gently, yet firmly admonished me for running out into the street without looking. He told me how scared he was when he saw me run in front of his car like I had. His passenger also spoke out of concern. I almost cried for these fine young men who I had carelessly put through this scary ordeal. He made me promise him that I would never do that again. I did. And I haven't. Somebody cared!

When my sister and I were eight or nine years old, my mother cornrowed our hair for the first time. I was mortified!

I hated it. Not because it looked bad. My mother could have made a living cornrowing hair. She was incredibly good at it! But we had never had our hair in a style that was so radical before. Our neighbor, Mrs. Bockums pressed our hair, or my mom would put two pig tails in our hair. During play, my sister and I would tie our white sweaters to our heads pretending we had long blond hair. Jerking our heads around, imitating the white women we'd seen in beauty commercials. Now, with our hair neatly cornrowed, my mother demanded that we walk the several blocks to, and from the store to get her some items. As we began that ill-fated walk, a young black man yelled from across the street, "Hey little sisters! I love your hair!" He had the biggest grin on his face, with his fist in the air. He genuinely liked our hair! *What?* From that moment on, I never again felt shame about the hairstyle that black women have been proudly sporting since the beginning of time. His compliment did more for my self-esteem than he will ever know. Somebody cared!

It was the sixties and hippies reigned supreme. Our camp counselors were the quintessential hippie group if I'd ever seen one. They took us on many trips to the mountains of Colorado during the summer. They meant well, but they had no clue about young children in their care. We were on a mountain hike on this day. Most of the campers had run ahead with the other counselors, while my sister and I brought up the rear with one of our male counselors. As we made the climb, the snow on the ground began to make my feet cold. Nobody told us that this mountain was snowcapped in the middle of summer. We had on shorts and sandals! The higher we went, the colder it got. And my feet were freezing! Each toe felt like a little ice cube. I started to complain. My sister didn't seem to be bothered. Maybe she had sneakers on, I don't remember. My counselor told me to turn around and go back to the van. Just follow the path we'd come from. I turned and began my descent back down the mountain *by myself*. I'd hung in there for quite some time, anxious to reach the top, but the snow-capped terrain was not gonna let me be great. I had a way to go to get back to the bottom, by myself. After a while, I began to cry. I was cold and scared. A family of five or six people stopped me. They were dressed for the occasion—long sleeved sweaters, jackets, long pants, boots, backpacks and walking sticks. They told me to sit down on the ledge. "Stop crying. You'll be alright." Someone pulled out half of a peanut butter & jelly sandwich and handed it to me. They stayed with me and chatted amongst themselves as I ate my sandwich, fighting back the tears, and wiping the snot that was making its descent onto my sandwich. They were so friendly and patient with me, that my fear left. When I finished eating, they reassured me that I would be at the bottom in no time. Just follow the path. They turned to go up, as I turned to go down. After a while, the warmth of their kindness dissipated, and I was cold and scared once more. Those tears streamed down my face, and I was in a full-blown bawl as a man and his dog neared me. He, like the others told me to sit on the ledge and to stop crying. He pulled out a container of water and handed it to me. He stood silently as I finished drinking. He reassured me that I was close to the end. "Take your time and follow the path!" he said as he wished me well and went up the mountain. I did as he said, and finally reached the bottom of that cloudy, snow-capped mountain! It was so sunny and warm at the bottom, as I made my way to the unlocked van. I hopped in the back and waited — by myself, for everyone else to reappear. I was never happier when they finally did. Those strangers didn't have to help me. They could have done me harm, but they were so nice instead. Somebody cared!

We were on a high school trip to New York to see a play. We had a couple of hours to kill, so our chaperones allowed us to roam around the streets of Manhattan. My sister and I were walking with two friends when two, very tall, dreadlocked men came out of nowhere. One grabbed my left arm, and the other, my right arm. They quickly walked me, with the other three girls in tow, across the street. I had no idea where I was going with these two strange men. I was so naive. Out of nowhere, our class adviser, Mr. French, appeared with another female teacher. "Where are you taking her?" Mr. French was half the height of these two dudes. "Do you know them?" he asked me. "No." Maybe they were merchants and wanted me to buy something. I don't know. "Get your hands off of her!" The two dudes left without an argument. And Mr. French lectured me about going off with strangers. I saw him a few years ago. He still remembered that incident so many decades ago. He was my hero! Somebody cared!

I was nineteen, and headed to Fort Wayne, Indiana to visit friends. It was the wee hours of the morning, and I was sitting in the Greyhound Bus station in Cleveland, Ohio, waiting for the next bus to my destination. Two gentlemen walked up to me. They were so bubbly, and friendly for this time of morning I thought. "Have you ever been to Cleveland before?" they asked. "No." I said. They tag teamed me about their city and how badly I needed to see it. I glanced at the door. It was pitch black outside. But before I realized it, I was up and walking with them towards the exit. When we got to the door, they continued to convince me to go outside. A loud voice that only I could hear, said, *do not go outside!* I peered to my left and then to my right. Not a creature was stirring, not even a mouse. Only cars lined the street in front of the almost empty station. Just then, a loud, angry voice that we all could hear, said, "Get away from her!" Those dudes quickly disappeared into the dark night. "Come here!" Said the rotund man in the Greyhound uniform. When I got close enough, he said sternly, "Your bus is the 4425 headed for Fort Wayne and leaves at 3:15 a.m. You sit down, and don't talk to anybody. When your bus gets here, you get on it and don't get off until you get to Fort Wayne. Do you hear?" "Yes." I said, as I nodded my head up and down. I did exactly what he told me. And when my bus came, he called me over to get on it. "Remember what I said!" He was serious. A father figure. My guardian angel in the flesh! I shudder to think what would have happened to me if no one cared enough to intervene that night. On the way back home from this trip, I had a little layover in Pittsburgh, Pennsylvania. Unlike my wait in Cleveland, it was the middle of the day, and very sunny outside. This Greyhound Bus Station was super crowded, bustling with travelers. I was sitting on a bench eating a PB & J sandwich when I saw him. Out of the corner of my eye, I could see him slowly, steadily walking towards me. He was *fine*! He was wearing a long, multicolored maxi coat, like the one I'd seen in those 70's black exploitation flicks. His hair was in cornrows. He was handsome, with a gorgeous smile. He was probably in his late twenties, maybe early thirties. I quickly looked away, remembering what Mr. Greyhound had told me in Cleveland. He walked right up to me and stopped. Right in front of me. He was smiling so broadly. "Hello," he spoke. He was smooth, like whipped butter. I uttered a shy, hi. Just then, a man's voice from two seats away, said, "Go on away from here and leave her alone." It wasn't the kind of voice you wanted to mess with. Mr. Maxi Coat, however, didn't move quickly. He never removed his gaze on me, or his smile, as he walked away very slowly. I couldn't stop staring at him. He was so brazen and seemingly fearless. Did I have a sign that read *Runaway* on my forehead? This time, my savior was a grandfather type in overalls. I hadn't noticed him before he spoke. There were no words spoken between us. I finished eating my sandwich and eventually made it safely back home. Somebody—no, *two* somebodies, cared!

Sometime during undergrad, my girlfriend and I decided to go dancing at a club in Philly. We lived in Camden, so we took the Speedline and walked the few blocks. When we got there, the entrance fee was a dollar more than we thought. My friend was the voice of reason, "C'mon Tracy, let's go home." We had just enough money for the Speedline and the club. I hadn't come all that way just to turn back around. "We can get a dollar from somebody inside." Well, let me tell you I must've asked everybody. All the guys I danced with, the girls in the bathroom, maybe even the bartender. Nobody had a dollar to spare! When we left, we were still a dollar short. We could have put our coins together and bought one ticket, but no, I was on a roll with the bad advice. "Let's jump the turnstile. Nobody will know." It was about two a.m. and the station was deserted. We were the only ones on the train. We got off on Broadway and walked up the steps. And there he was, Camden's finest—all six feet three inches of him! "We saw y'all on the monitor." My heart leapt out my chest and scurried down the steps. My knees started to buckle, and I was frozen. I think I stopped breathing, too. I was too scared to look at my girlfriend. "Come with me I'll take you home." Huh? My heart and my breathing came back, my knees cooperated, and we timidly got into the patrol car. When the officer pulled up in front of a deserted building and told us to get out, I panicked again. My friend and I looked at each other, what in the world? "C'mon get out so I can take your picture." He had a professional grade camera. He took two pictures of me and two pictures of my friend. He had to tell us to smile. Why is he taking our picture? Is he gonna arrest us or what? I was never happier to see my grandmother's house when he pulled up. He admonished us for jumping the turnstile and told me that I could pick up our pictures from him at the station in a couple of weeks. The pictures came out nice. Somebody cared!

I was in my twenties and was having a conversation with a friend about drugs — crack cocaine. He'd been a drug dealer before we met. Sometime during this conversation, I heard myself say, "I wanna try some coke. I want to know what it is everybody is all hyped about!" It was the dumbest thing I have ever asked for. As if I would be immune to the harrowing effects of this destroying drug. The next thing he said was the absolute best. "No, Tracy. You'll get addicted." Thank you for that. Somebody cared!

Six months after my husband's death, I'd gotten some bad news that devastated me. One night as I lay in bed, I contemplated suicide. I had put all my husband's medications in a shopping bag and placed it atop his closet shelf. I remember thinking that if life got to be too hard, this was going to be my way out. It was the wee hours of the morning when I was considering how to carry this thing out without my sleeping children suffering any harm. My mother lived too close; she would get here too soon. My sister lived further away, but she might call my mother, or worse, the police! As tears streamed down my face, I was torn about my children. I didn't want them in a house with a corpse trying to fend for themselves. They were so young, and so little. Suddenly a voice spoke. "Call Sister Henry!" Sister Henry was a widow from my church. She was also a registered nurse. After my husband's death, she had introduced herself to me and took me out to lunch and shared her testimony with me. Her husband died while in the military. They were only in their twenties when he died. They had a baby daughter. Sister Henry was now close to retirement, and her daughter had a daughter. It was so dark in my bedroom, I couldn't see my hand in front of me, but I was able to find her number and call her. "Hello?" Her voice was almost a whisper. My ears were ringing from the loudness roaring inside of me. Everything inside of me had to get quiet for me to hear her. My words were incoherent I was crying so hard. "The lawyers said they are not going to take my case. They'd had my documents for six months and they said, it isn't conclusive that he died of negligence. I didn't want to live anymore. Life is so disappointing." The law firm had me fill out paperwork about disbursement of funds and told me how they had successfully represented a woman in a similar lawsuit. I just knew my case was cut and dried. I was so disappointed

. I was crying so hard, I don't know how Sister Henry understood anything I'd said, but her next words were, "Tracy, I want you to get the bag of medications and go into the bathroom. Open each bottle and pour the pills into the toilet and flush the toilet when you are finished. I'll wait here on the phone. Go 'head." Her voice was so low and calm, as if she'd been waiting for my call. Like a robot, I did exactly as she told me. I was a bit disappointed that she hadn't told me to throw the pills in the trash. I would have retrieved them later. But not the toilet! She ministered to me that dark, early morning and promised to come over later that day. I sat on the floor, looking up at Sister Henry seated on my couch as she firmly yet lovingly told me that suicide was not the answer. I had two children who needed me. They no longer had a father, and what would happen to them without a mother as well? I had to live for them, she said. I loved my babies more than I loved myself. They are who I was thinking of earlier that morning in my torment. Her love and selflessness helped me realize the love Elohim has for me. Somebody cared!

I have never been as low as I was the night that I wanted to end my life. My husband's pills were my security. And Yahuah knew exactly who to connect me with to talk me "off the ledge." What a blessing Sister Henry was for me and for my children! Thank you, Sister Henry!

My grandmother told me once, that when she separated from her husband, she prayed and asked the Lord to spare her life until her children were grown. Not only did our Heavenly Father spare her to see her children grown, but she lived to see grown grandchildren, and great-grandchildren! Yah blessed her beyond what she had asked. That has been my prayer as well. Especially with a disabled adult son who cannot live independently yet. Thank you, Lord, for your continual abode with me and my children!

Somebody cared, and it has always been my Heavenly Father! Hallelujah!

"By this I know that thou favourest (are well pleased with) me, because mine enemy doth not triumph (shout in applause) over me."

Psalm 41:11 KJV

Jeffery and Tracy Fowler

Tracy – college days

James' graduation 1987

Tracy with twin sister in uncle's coupe

Tracy with mom in Denver, CO

Tracy's mom with stepdad on Army base 1964

Grandma Mattie

Daughter Charis 2001

Son Chayil 2001

References

1. John G Kruis. Ryrie Study Bible: Quick Scripture Reference for Counseling, Expanded Edition. 2013, p. 160

2. https://pastorpaul.net/

3. https://www.cdc.gov/mmwr/volumes/68/wr/mm6843a3.htm

Appendix

Recommended Reading and Follows

The following is a list of books and social media pages that have helped me gain a more practical sense about living the saved life.

1. **Cepher – means scroll, book, or even a numbered writing.** Includes eighty-seven inspired and historical books in the chronological order of their writing. Transliterates the names of the Father, Son, and Holy Spirit without substitution. Omitted in other translations, the Aleph Tav has been restored over 10,000 times. www.cepher.net

2. http://www.truthunedited.com/

3. @2larryjohnson7 on Instagram

4. Pastor Stephen Darby of Destined Ministries https://www.youtube.com/user/sldskd88

5. When People Are BIG and GOD Is Small, Overcoming Peer Pressure Codependency, and the Fear of Man by Edward T. Welch, Presbyterian and Reformed Publishing Company, P.O. Box 817, Phillipsburg, New Jersey 08865-0817

6. The Red Sea Rules, 10 God-Given Strategies for Difficult Times by Robert J Morgan, 2001, Thomas Nelson Inc, Publisher in association with the literary agency of Alive Communications, 7680 Goddard Street, Suite 200, Colorado Springs, CO 80920

7. The Battle Is The Lord's, Waging Victorious Spiritual Warfare, by Dr. Tony Evans, 1998, Moody Press Publishers, Chicago, Illinois

8. Shepherding A Child's Heart by Tedd Tripp, 1995, Shepherd Press, P.O. Box 24, Wapwallopen, PA 18660

9. Rebuilding What The Enemy Almost Destroyed, Practical Insights From The Book Of Nehemiah, by Paul Sheppard, 2017, Xulon Press, 2301 Lucien Way #415, Maitland, FL 32751

10. Getting Over The Blues, A Woman's Guide to Fighting Depression, by Leslie Vernick, 2005, Harvest House Publishers, Eugene, Oregon 97402

About The Author

With 35 years of experience as an educator, new author Tracy Fowler has touched the lives of many, from all ages and all backgrounds. A dedicated and faithful member of the Baptist faith, this widow is the mother of two young adults, a deaconess, and member of the outreach and counseling ministry at her home church.

CPSIA information can be obtained
at www.ICGtesting.com
Printed in the USA
LVHW011650231221
707030LV00011B/1122